# FARM OF MY CHILDHOOD

By

Mary  Roberts

Ille terrarum mihi praeter omnis angulus ridet
(Horace)

(that corner of the world smiles for me
more than anywhere else)

The
Book
Castle

First published November 1991
by
The Book Castle
12 Church Street
Dunstable
Bedfordshire LU5 4RU

Reprinted April 1992

ISBN 1-871199-50-6

Front cover:     'Little gleaners, near Pulloxhill, Bedfordshire.'

Back cover:      detail from 'Over the stepping stones.'

Both watercolours by H J Sylvester Stannard, 1870–1951,
reproduced by arrangement with Kenulf Gallery,
Winchcombe.

Computer typeset by 'Keyword', Aldbury, Hertfordshire.
Printed and bound by Inprint, Hitchin, Hertfordshire.

# CONTENTS

## Part One

## AUTOBIOGRAPHY

## Part Two

## HISTORY

## Part Three

## APPENDICES

❖ ❖ ❖ ❖ ❖

❖ ❖ ❖ ❖ ❖

**To my Mother and Father**

**WALTER & EVA COLE**

**with love**

## THE AUTHORESS

Mary Roberts was born at Priestley Farm, Flitwick, in Bedfordshire, in 1925, leaving only after her Father died in 1947. This book tells the story of her life on the farm, and farming methods, during these twenty-two years.

With her husband, Peter, she lives now in an old Sarsen stone cottage, in a quiet hamlet, tucked away in a fold of the Marlborough Downs. They have Bonnie, a black Labrador bitch, and Benjamin, a twenty-three year old donkey who was hand-reared by them from two days old.

Much of their leisure time is spent walking on the downs, or tending their cottage garden, which glows with colour and is visited by many species of birds and butterflies.

# AUTHOR'S ACKNOWLEDGEMENTS

Over the lengthy period whilst I have been collecting material for this book, I have received help from many individuals. Firstly Peter, my husband, who encouraged me from the beginning; my friend, Eileen Jenkins, without whose help and hard work this book would have been unreadable; Joan Stevens, who put the punctuation, etc. in the right places; Vivienne Evans, who made many sympathetic suggestions about the text, especially the history section; Nigel Baldock for his patience and help with the maps, and Samantha Pratt for her meticulous copying of them.

Also my thanks to all my relations and friends who knew Priestley Farm and took such an interest in the book throughout the years; the Peat family, Ron and Stan and their sisters Cis and Nellie for their wonderful letters and stories of Priestley long ago; the late Mrs B Carr and the late Mrs D Carr for the blacksmith background; Mary Pressland for her lacework; Dicky Cox for all her natural history notes; Tom Norris for the information on gamekeeping; land girls Jean and Betty Pearson for their notes; Mr and Mrs E Bonner and Mr and Mrs G Little, now living at Priestley; and all the people who wrote to me with interesting information or provided photographs.

In addition I am grateful to the staff of Marlborough Library, who dealt with such efficiency with my many requests for books outside their area, and also to the staff of the Bedfordshire County Record Office for their help and permission to reproduce various documents; similarly the Marquess of Tavistock and the Trustees of Bedford Estates, along with Mr K Fadden, Chairman of the Ampthill and District Archaeological and Local History Society. I am indebted to its present editor, Betty Chambers, for allowing me to base some extracts on articles in the Bedfordshire Magazine. I also acknowledge information from Mr A W Bennett, Production Manager of Streetley Minerals Limited, and from Anglian Water, Cambridge, about the River Flit.

Certain books were especially valuable. For general background, Joyce Godber's 'History of Bedfordshire' and the 'Victoria County History of Bedfordshire' (vol. 3). In specialist areas, several volumes published by the Bedfordshire Historical Record Society – 'The Diary of a Bedfordshire Squire' (vol. 66), 'The 1830 Riots' (vol. 57), 'The Court of Augmentation for Bedfordshire' (vol. 64), 'The Bedfordshire

Schoolchild' (vol. 67), and 'The Bedfordshire Farm Worker in the Nineteenth Century' (vol. 60). On the immediately local area, 'Flitwick, the Story of an Old Bedfordshire Village', by Rev. J L Ward Petley, and 'Flitwick, a Short History', published by the Ampthill and District Archaeological and Local History Society.

To all these people and sources, and if I have forgotten to mention any please forgive me, and to Priestley Farm, I give all my love and grateful thanks.

# PROLOGUE

I have written this story of Priestley Farm remembering how fortunate I was to be born and brought up among loving and caring country folk, on a farm before and during the Second World War.

Farming today is so very different from the days of my childhood. Then it was hard manual work for men and women, but for us, the children, there were long days of pleasure among the fields, woods, streams and animals. When not at school we were allowed much freedom, as long as we kept out of the men's way and were on time for meals, with hands hastily washed. We had a set time for bed, but otherwise were left to our own devices.

During the haymaking and harvest we were allowed to help on the farm, leading the horses and driving the empty carts from stack to field. Today, with all the high-powered machinery, there is too much danger for children to play in the farmyard. In fact, the farmyward no longer exists, as it was in my childhood. No hay or corn stacks to slide down, although this was forbidden and there was trouble if we were caught doing it, nor are there any great carthorses to ride or delightful places for hide-and-seek. Priestley was isolated in those days but we were never lonely. Friends walked or cycled from nearby villages in school holidays, or we made our own entertainment.

In the following pages I hope you will accompany me as I describe my memories. There were happy days and, of course, sad days, but I hope the love and happiness of our 'wonderful days of Priestley' shine through.

Although I have dedicated this book to my parents, Eva and Walter Cole whom I remember with love, I include all the men and women, those whom I knew and those long before my time, who worked the lands of Priestley, so making this book possible.

For the history of the Manor of Priestley I have, in the words of John Speed, '… put my sickle into other men's corne …'. I hope they will not mind too much.

MARY ROBERTS
January, 1991

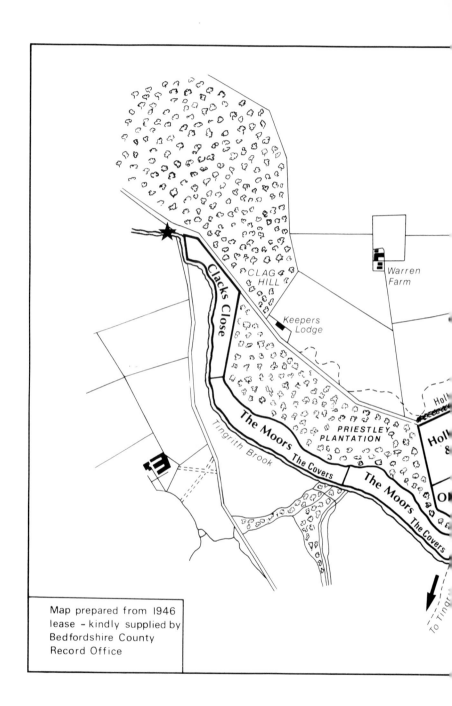

CLAG HILL

Clacks Close

Warren Farm

Keepers Lodge

The Moors

The Covers

PRIESTLEY PLANTATION

Tingrith Brook

Holl

Hol &

O

The Moors

The Covers

To Tingr

Map prepared from 1946 lease – kindly supplied by Bedfordshire County Record Office

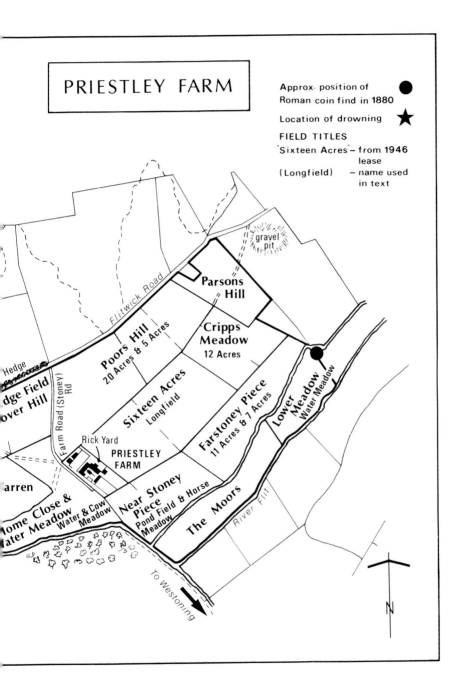

## PART ONE

# Autobiography

*This watercolour depicts Thrupp End Farm, Lidlington, where my husband, Peter, was born in 1919. It has been owned by Peter's relatives for many decades, and is thought to have been painted for them by one of the Stannards, the famous Bedfordshire family of watercolourists.*

*It shows a haymaking scene in the field where various members of the Stannard and Roberts families, and others, regularly played mixed hockey matches against other Bedfordshire teams at the turn of the century.*

Chapter 1

# Wonderful Days of Priestley

I have read somewhere that a child who had listened to classical music from birth and through its formative years would grow up with a deep and lasting love and understanding of that music. Whether this is true I do not know, but I do know that the first sounds that greeted me on my arrival early one May morning, in the front bedroom of Priestley Farm, would have been the age-old farmyard noises of cows lowing and horses stamping on the cobble stones in their stables. I grew up with these sounds, which are music to my ears, and the love of the country sounds and ways will remain with me always.

My Father, Walter Cole, rented Priestley, a farm of nearly three hundred acres, and moved into the farmhouse from Hillcot Farm, New Road, Maulden, in 1914 with his wife, Eva, and their two children, Margaret aged six and Alfred aged four. Richard was born in 1919 and I (Mary) was born in May 1925 at Priestley Farm.

*Mother and Father with my Godparents, William and Mabel Walker, in the dicky seat of Father's first car outside Priestley Farm House, early 1920s.*

The house was large and rambling, with a fair-sized garden and tennis court and an orchard of old apple and pear trees, one very old damson tree, bent almost double, and an old yellow gage in the hedgerow. There were two cottages and many well-built brick farm buildings.

The ground varied from peaty moorland to a sandy soil, and various crops were grown – wheat, oats, barley, potatoes, peas, marrows, beans, beetroot, sugar beet, mangles, cabbage, brussels sprouts, parsley, hay from the water meadows and lucerne (a green feed for cattle).

There were sheep, a herd of milking cows, beef cattle, pigs and horses for work on the farm. Gradually, tractors and lorries took over many of the jobs done by the horses, but, thankfully, some were still kept for light work on the land. My Father hated the heavy tractors on his light market-garden land, so I was lucky enough to grow up with those wonderful animals.

I was fond of all the farm animals, but most of all I loved the great farm horses, those 'gentle giants'. Their names seemed to be the same as those on other farms, Boxer, Prince, Bonny, Blossom, Lady, Captain, Turpin, Daisy, Taffy, Shorty, Tinker and Kit or Joe for the ponies that

*Shorty and Tinker grazing in the horse meadow. Beyond them is Westoning Park. They were the last two horses used by us at Priestley Farm.*

pulled the milk float. Blossom was one of my great favourites, a bright bay mare with a pink diamond on her soft-moustached nose. She and I shared many a lollipop as I sat in her manger.

I have always thought that a manger was a cosy place for the baby Jesus to have lain in. The mother cats on the farm found them safe and warm for their kittens, watched over by the large gentle eyes of the horses or cows. As I grew up, the stables were full of horses. The cows came in from the meadows, night and morning, to be milked by hand by Tom Parker and his son, Jack. The milk ran hissing into shining pails, frothing to the top. It was then poured into the cooler (aluminium pipes with cold water running through them), and then into churns. The churns were picked up night and morning from the farm by Mr Harrold, who had a milk round in Flitwick, later taken over by Mr Warr, his son-in-law. The milk float was pulled by a rather cross-looking black pony called Ada. The cows were mixed breeds of Shorthorns, Red Polls and Friesians. All had names, – Poppy, Amy, Nancy, Bluebell, Daisy, Buttercup, Madcap and Ida, being some of the names I remember. Nancy was a great favourite. I would ride on her back as she walked in from the meadow,

*Author with Nancy, my favourite cow, on which I loved to be given a ride from the field to the cow shed at milking time.*

and most of the cows were quiet enough for me to chain up whilst they ate their food. What a tempting mixture they had, all made up on the mixing-house floor, broken-up cattle cake, chopped mangels, chaff, bran, flaked maize, and soaked sugar beet piled in layers and then mixed with a large shovel into a heap, then put into bags and taken to the cowshed and ladled out with a bowl into the mangers.

In summer, there was cool, green freshly-cut lucerne, which is somewhat similar to clover, growing to a height of about three feet, with green leaves and clusters of small purple flowers. Animals love it. Lucerne is also known as Alfalfa, which is Spanish from the Arabic, alfasfasah - best fodder. The cattle also had green maize (commonly called corn on the cob) cut before the cobs form. The thick fleshy stems were crunched down with enjoyment. In winter, there was sweet meadow hay to munch through the long dark hours.

Some of the cows slept in their cowsheds and were bedded down with golden wheat straw. I loved to peer over the door, seeing them all snug and warm in the lamplight, their sweet milky breath blending with the lingering scent of hay filling the night air. I had to be very quiet and still in order not to frighten them.

In 1943, an Alfa Laval Electric Milking Machine was installed, and one of the loose boxes was turned into a proper dairy for cooling milk and the old lean-to shed by the scullery was dismantled. Milk records were kept of night and morning milking, a job I had to do at times which always seemed to coincide with a dance the night before, and still half asleep on the stool I wrote down the weighed milk, aided and abetted by the helpful milkers, so that Father thought I had been wide awake and 'with it' throughout the milking. I was not keen on the milking machine, as anything mechanical I viewed with mistrust. However, it made life easier for those who had to do the milking and the cows soon got used to it. The cost of the machine, entered in Father's ledger, was £110.4s.9d. Also, about that time, A Lister & Co. Milk Cooler was purchased at a cost of £5.9s.10d.

I have previously mentioned that horses were my great love, and I well remember one evening, when I was very young, a dapper little man, leading the most beautiful creature I had ever seen, a shire horse stallion, came to the kitchen door. The stallion's coat shone so that you could almost see y our face in the gleaming massive quarters; his thick and crested neck arched as he looked down at me, each plait of his mane topped with straw and ribbon, and those great feet spread about with silky white feather (hair). Around his barrel-shaped body was a blue and red circingle (band) with brass rings. His bridle was blinkerless and had shining brass buckles. I begged Father to buy him. Never had I wanted anything so much. Needless to say he was not for sale, as he was one of the travelling stallions going round to various farms. His progeny from some favoured farm mare would quite often be proudly shown at the local agricultural show the following year.

One Spring morning, much to my delight, out Suffolk Punch mare, Daisy, produced a little chestnut filly foal. They named her Queenie. I saw her with her proud mother among the daisies in the orchard before I was marched off to school. On my return, mother and foal were missing. Tragically, Queenie had died. Not all my tears could bring her back.

I cannot remember when Father purchased his first tractor. No doubt my brothers were wild with delight. There is mention in his ledgers of work done with a tractor in October 1938 - 'Potato Lifting, Wages to men and women £7.13s.6d. Lorry for carting same £1.0s.0d. and use of implements and tractor 10s.0d.'

In November 1941, a new tractor from Standen & Son cost £437.10s.0d., and in December 1942, a Massey-Harris tractor from Martin & Sons cost £365. Other implements purchased included, in 1941 a Hay Loader, £48.0s.0d., Potato Digger £108.0s.0d., Trailer £76.0s.0d., Plough £44.5s.0d. In 1943, Martin & Son supplied a Binder for £153.0s.0d.

Although Father had moved with the times and used tractors at Priestley and for contract work for other farmers, he still preferred to use horses on his light land. At Maulden, where his land was light market-garden land, he kept two horses in the charge of Mr Alfred King, the horse keeper. I remember Prince, a grey, and Bonny, a dark bay. Sometimes they came to Priestley when another pair of horses were needed. I don't think Mr King really approved of his beloved charges in the Priestley Stables.

The horses also did contract work, and their charges were as follows:

| | | |
|---|---|---|
| 1942. | One team ploughing all day - £1.15s.0d. | |
| 1943-45. | One team ploughing all day - £1.17s.6d. | |
| 1946. | One team ploughing all day - £2.5s.0d. | |
| 1947. | One man, 2 horses, 1 day - £2.10s.0d. | |

Father sometimes bought his horses from Mr Copperwheat at Ampthill. Some were successful, others a problem. One he bought from another dealer worked well in chain harness, but would not move in the shafts of a cart. He was found to have a weak back, but he stayed at Priestley doing light work for the rest of his life. His name was Turpin, a bay with a fine curling moustache.

My Father also farmed at Biggleswade where, again, the soil was light market-garden land. There were also horses there, light-legged (not heavy shire) but strong, suitable for market garden work. He had purchased a sixteen hands, dark, almost black, light-boned, hunter-type horse, to work on the land. This horse had a beautiful head and was thought to have been someone's favourite hunter who had been broken to harness and sold on. His name was Black Jim and he had a mind of his own. He would pull the cart willingly with a light load; one bag more, and he refused to budge. The men got fed up with him and he was sent to Priestley. As soon as I saw him I loved him. My pony being lame, I begged Father to let me hunt him. He turned out to be the best hunter I ever rode. He still did his share of farm work; horse hoe-harrowing, etc., and carting feed to the cattle. But no heavy work. After a set-to one harvest, being short of a horse for carting the corn, they had put Black Jim to a trolley and carted a couple of loads of sheaves with him. Suddenly, with an empty trolley, he called it a day and refused to move. The men were tired and cross and I heard them shouting at him. I rushed over and, big-headed, said, 'I know he would move for me'. Father arrived at that moment, saw me in tears, the men understandably cross and irritated with me, the horse's head down, motionless, and when told of the situation he just said, 'If Mary thinks she can move him, let her'. How I wished I had kept my mouth shut. The men had by then all gathered round and I took Jim by his bridle and said, 'Come on, old man,' and on he walked. Father had him taken out of the trolley at once, and he was never asked to pull a harvest cart again. He carried me across country for many years, and I took him with me when I married. He was in my care for the rest of his life, and the sadness of the day when he was put down through old age and failing health remains with me to this day.

There was also a wholesale business which was started in the Borough Market, London, in the late 1800s by my grandfather, Alfred Cole, and my Father, who was born at Biggleswade in Bedfordshire. The produce at one time was sent up to London via the railway, and there would be lines of horses and carts queueing up at Biggleswade station in the late afternoon to unload their bags and boxes on to the goods train for delivery in London early the next morning. Later on, my Father owned several lorries which would collect the produce grown not only by himself, but by other growers in the district, who would contact him to pick up so many bags or boxes of produce which would be sold on commission. The amount of produce varied at different times of the year, and often two or more lorries would be needed to collect the produce piled by the roadside of various fields and villages. Often it was collected in the smaller vehicles, brought back to Priestley, and reloaded on to the larger lorries. the loading and neatness of packing knobbly bags and bulging boxes, and the deftness of the knotted rope to make all secure before the lorry left early the next morning for the Borough Market, never ceased to amaze me. The men who loaded these lorries had their skills handed down to them from those who had loaded wagons with hay and sheaves of corn from the fields to travel through narrow, humpy gateways to the stackyard. There might be a frantic message from someone who thought his bags or boxes of produce had been forgotten, but, as far as I can remember, there was never a message to say a lorry had shed its load. All the produce had to be clean and carefully packed, although some was of better quality and better packed than others. The weather also played an important part, as it does to this day. No one wanted lettuce when the temperature dropped, and a mild pre-Christmas spell was no good for sprouts. Deep freezing today has changed the vegetable market. But there is nothing quite like freshly grown vegetables and fruit.

Many acres of peas were grown at Priestley, and women (known as the 'peasing' women) would be picked up by lorry from the surrounding villages. A message would be left previously at various points (probably local pubs) that 'Cole' require pea-pickers on a certain date. The lorry-load of 'peasing' women was a mixture of noise and colour. Some women took along their babies and young children. All had a low stool or chair, hats or scarves hopefully to keep off the sun, and old coats in case of rain or cold. They sang, laughed, swore or cried according to their age or creed. But how they worked. They pulled up the vine, laid it over their knees, stripped off the fat-podded peas into the bucket, which they emptied into hessian bags which had 'Alfred Cole and Son' printed on them. The bags were weighed by a man in charge of the weighing machine, which was a platform stacked with weights on one side and another platform on the other side on which the bags or boxes were placed and a ticket given. Tickets of different colours were given for each field, or batch, of peas, recording the price per bag, which had been arranged with the women before picking started. The women often stuck the tickets under their garters to keep them safe. The bags were stacked in a heap ready for collection by horse and cart, or lorry, for market.

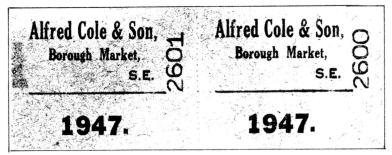

*Tickets given to the women gathering peas, for each bag of peas gathered, which were exchanged for cash at the end of the peasing session.*

Around about four o'clock the women, with children, prams, buckets and stools, would pile into the lorry for their return journey home. Mostly they were paid at the end of the day, but some would wait and cash their tickets at the end of the week. It was hard work, but a way of supplementing the housekeeping money for many country women.

One person I particularly remember was Emma Smith, who lived at Tingrith. She came across the brook to help Mother in the house and took care of me at times. She was a strong woman who never seemed to tire. During the summer she worked in the field, pea-picking. However early one went into the field, Emma was always there first, sitting on her stool and picking the peas from the vine, her bucket almost full. As I grew older, I often rode over on a Sunday morning to the house she and her husband owned. There, in her kitchen, Emma would be baking delicious little cakes, of which I was given a sample.

There was one group of men on the farm who usually worked piecework, which meant they were paid an arranged price for a piece of work, i.e. so much for hand hoeing or singling beet, or such small crops, so much per bag for brussels sprouts. Now, many of these jobs are done by machines, but in my day they were done by this gang of men; some of their names I remember, George Scott, Jim Oakley, Alf Pool, Charley Oakley and Bert Parker. They must have crawled many miles during the seasons, though the picking of frozen or wet brussels sprouts is no fun! They wore sacks around their legs and backs for extra protection. I so well remember them telling me that after the first few minutes their hands were not cold. The sprouts were packed into 28lb bags, and weighed with a steel-yard (a spring weighing machine), which they had attached to their belts. Then the full bags (nearly always wet) were carried on their shoulders to the end of the row to await collection for market.

In early spring the brussels and cabbage plants were planted out in rows with a dibber. A dibber is a tool with a short handle, the stem coming to a point about five inches long with which to make a hole to take a small plant. Boxes of plants were placed at intervals along marked lines, and a youngster (sometimes me) had to hand out a bundle of plants to the men who, skilfully, dibber in one hand and a bundle of plants in the other, planted those rows like clockwork. The one who handed out the plants from the boxes had to make sure that a bundle of plants was ready within reach as soon as the man planting our was empty-handed. A cry of 'here boy' made sure you moved at the double. How often I have seen one of the men straighten his back and take from his 'weskit' (waistcoat) pocket, a heavy silver encased pocket watch with chain attached, and, glancing over to the LMS Railway line, about two miles away, proclaim the such-and-such express was running late, or to time, as the case may be. Today, my husband checks Concorde flying high above our Wiltshire cottage by his wrist watch, and makes the same remark as did those men working in the Priestley fields.

Some time after my brother Richard's death in 1985, my sister-in-law, Maisie, gave me a chest full of my Father's old Priestley ledgers, etc., which had been stored away in an outhouse. Some were damp and musty, but on my reading through them, they brough back memories of the office at Priestley Farm over whose door the martins returned each spring to build their nests with mud from nearby ponds and yards – one thing Priestley was never short of was mud. Their blue-black heads, with bright eyes, would peep down on us as we entered the office, which was a square room with a window overlooking the yard, a large cupboard, a small fireplace and a door leading to a back room in which were kept animal medicines and some of the vegetable seeds, such as carrots, parsley, beet, etc. The office itself was quite cosy in winter, with the fire and a smell of leather-bound books, ink and liniments.

A succession of clerks helped with the bookwork. My sister, Margaret, when she left Howard College, Bedford, was a great help to Father and enjoyed the office work, and continued to help right up to her death in 1938. I was supposed to follow on but, alas, and to Father's disgust, figures were, and always have been, a complete mystery to me. One of the earlier clerks was a Mr Arthur Carr, whose father kept the Flitwick Post Office. But the first one I remember was Willie Parsons. His father kept the grocer's shop on Station Square, Flitwick. He took great pains to help me with my lessons, and did delightful drawings to amuse me. Others followed, and the last one was a Mr Bagnall.

Each morning my Father would telephone the Borough Market, London, for a report on the vegetables sold early that morning by his salesman. Father would then record in his telephone and day books not only vegetable prices but notes on the weather and other snippets of news. I have included some of the entries of those books in this chapter (the prices of vegetables are approximate).

The first of the books began in 1933 and on Tuesday, June 6th, after Whitsun, there was a heatwave with temperatures reaching ninety degrees in the shade! The market was full of lettuce at three shillings (fifteen pence) per dozen, parsley, rhubarb, beetroot and peas. Jersey potatoes made nine shilling (forty-five pence) a bag. The heatwave continued for the next few weeks, and crops began to dry up. The weather then turned stormy. A fire broke out in the Borough Market, upsetting the trade. At Priestley swede seed drilled on June 20th was washed out by the storm and had to be drilled again on June 26th. In 1935, on May 7th, the day after King George and Queen Mary's Silver Jubilee, my Father recorded that the weather was warm and sunny, and lettuce was selling well in the market.

We were all completely shattered by my sister, Margaret's death in July 1938. On that date, the 24th, Father wrote just one word in his book – 'Margaret'.

Easter Monday in 1939 fell on April 10th, and was very warm – the warmest Easter for several years. But on April 28th of that year the weather turned frosty with thick ice on the water-troughs. The variations in the weather dictated, as always, the market prices and the work carried out on the land.

The months leading up to the declaration of World War Two were worrying times for all. A peaceful settlement was hoped and prayed for but, on Friday, September 1st, Father wrote 'Weather dull, evacuation ordered of children in London. Uncertain whether to load vegetables or not'. Then, later that day, he wrote a message to a Mr Denny, one of his growers, 'Nothing sold. Advise stop loading. Will ring if any alteration'. On Saturday, September 2nd, there was no trade in the market. On Monday, September 4th, is written, 'War declared with Germany on Sunday. London nearly empty'. The following week trade in the market was very slow. On September 5th, the message to Mr Denny was to 'Go steady with parsley as the fish market has left London and at present we cannot find it'. On Wednesday, September 6th, there was an air raid warning, which brought the market to a standstill, with no vegetables coming in to the market. The weather remained fine and warm. Once the scare of air raids was over, the vegetables began to arrive in the market once more. They must have found the fish market again, because parsley was selling there at 3/- (15p) per dozen bunches.

The entries in the books continue: cabbages, peas, potatoes, marrows, rhubarb, lettuce, etc. giving their market prices. The state of the weather, on Monday April 22nd 1940, is noted. The first martins arrive, he heard the cuckoo on the 19th, and the weather was fine, with a light frost. The war news was bad, our troops in France being driven back to the coast. The evacuation from Dunkirk began. In the Borough Market, trading continued with plenty of vegetables arriving from Bedfordshire, either by lorry or, if any trucks were available, by rail, quite often arriving late. On Tuesday, June 25th, there was an air raid warning which again upset trade for a while. September that year came in hot and dry with crops needing rain. Fly was attacking the green-stuff, and cabbage plants were difficult to find. Then during the weekend of September 7th, air raids on London began. The weather was dry but cooler, and on September 11th another message to Mr Denny read, 'Load not arrived today. Very little trade. Several shops blown up. Do not load anything today. Parsley very bad trade. NO FISH!' The air raids continued. Produce quite often failing to reach the market. The weather for September is recorded as the driest time ever remembered.

In October, after sixteen weeks, rain came at last, but trade in the market remained slow. On December 30th, the lorry carrying the produce from Priestley to the Borough Market had trouble getting through as there were large fires burning in London.

On February 15th 1941, a bomb fell on the Borough Market, and the entry for that day states, (surprise, surprise), 'Nothing loaded'. No trade then, but by February 17th the Market was trading again, with turnips, parsley, savoy cabbage, carrots and sprouts. Spring arrived in spite of the dreadful air raids on London, and on May 12th the martins arrived once again to build their nests above the office door. Telephoning to London became almost impossible, as priority calls only were put through. To make life more difficult, the weather was cold and sleet fell. Spare parts for the tractors on the farm were difficult to obtain and there is written, on May 13th, a note for a contact breaker and fan-belt for a nine year-old Fordson tractor. On Saturday, May 17th, is the reply, 'The Beds. Auto Car Co. have not got the particular part you want and cannot get it as it is German, but if you break down completely they can probably fix you up!'

There are notes to remind my Father to send off log books and petrol applications for lorries, and notes to say where boxes of produce are to be picked up, mostly by some wayside field.

On June 6th, 1944 – D-DAY! The weather is recorded as cool and showery during the night after high winds. Then in written, 'Invasion of France', underlined. 'Not much trade'. Then, at the end of the month is the entry, 'London in a bad way owing to blitz by pilotless airplanes. Very few customers in the market'. Again on July 3rd, 'London is in a very bad way'. On August 8th, 'The weather warm and dry. A quieter night. No so many bombs. No customers in market'.

Tuesday, May 8th 1945, records, 'Weather mild. V E DAY', written in big letters. The next day, May 8th, 'Weather mild, thundery, holiday after V E Day. No one at work – weeds growing fast'. War or peace the weeds grow and care of the land must go on. Produce from the country must be gathered, packed and carted to the large towns and cities all over Britain.

And so the entries in my Father's books continued through the years until Monday, 3rd February 1947, when my brother, Richard, wrote, 'The death of my dearest Father took place this morning at 3.20am, at 42, de Parry's Avenue, Bedford, Mother, Alfred, Mary and myself being present to the last'.

Chapter Two

# Seasonal Events

## Hay Time

Hay time was an anxious time and most of the men disliked the job. So much to do in so little time. Hayseeds stick to sweating backs and the hay had to be taken just when it was ready. Often pouring rain would ruin a really good thick crop.

The old grass cutter would be pulled out from the shed, or from under a bush where it had rested since the last 'heysel'. Knives were sharpened, belts tightened, two steady horses harnessed and 'put to'. The horse keeper, lines (reins) in hand, would climb stiffly on to the iron seat on which he had previously placed a folded sack for comfort, and off they would rattle to the water meadows. Another horse and cart would follow with nosebags for the horses, the horse keeper's 'docky bag' (lunch bag or basket), extra knives for the machine and a stand and file for honing the knives to razor sharpness.

In a corner of the hayfield, under the shade of a twisted old hawthorn bush, all the gear would be unloaded, the lunch bag placed in the shade, and a bottle of cold tea, so loved by the farm workers, laid in the shallow waters of the brook. The spare team was tethered, until required, a few nuts tightened with a spanner, and all was ready for the first cut. The horses obeyed, willingly, both rein and spoken word and put their shoulders to the collar, and with knives chattering the team strode into the rippling grasses, leaving a swathe of cut meadow grasses, vetches, milkmaids, daisies and clovers, wilting in the sun, the sweet scent of their dying mingling with the sweat of the horses.

The hayfield was a wonderful place for us children. Hay houses could be made from the cut grass, and we needed no second bidding to take the basket of food prepared in the old kitchen to the men at work in the fields. We sat in the shade of that old tree and shared the men's food, watching fascinated as those bottles of cold tea (some still with tealeaves) were tilted upwards and the refreshing liquid poured down parched throats. The horses flung up their nosebags to get to the oats which had sunk to the bottom of the bag, stamped their hooves to be rid of the ever-persistent flies, and were thankful for the rest. Horses and men dozed for a short

14

while, and then it was back to the whirring chatter of the machine.

With a spell of fine weather the mowing would soon be done. The cut grass would then be raked into lines by the horse rake, an implement with shafts pulled by one horse, the operator sitting on the seat above the rake to drive the horse and at intervals to pull a lever which lifted the long tines gathering the cut grass into neat swathes, for the men to turn and toss the next day, and so making all that sweetness of grass and flowers into hay. The sun and the wind having dried the hay it was then put into heaps, 'haycocks', by the men with two-pronged forks. With the weather set fair, the hay was ready to be carted and stacked. Sometimes the hay was stacked in the field but nearly always carted to the stackyard. As soon as the dew was off the grass, horses and carts made their way to the field: the hay was pitched on to the cart and then taken back to the stackyard, where it was unloaded on to an elevator which carried it up onto the stack. The elevator was turned by a pony harnessed to a pole, which it pulled whilst walking in a circle; usually an old quiet pony was chosen for this job. They plodded round and round, resting between cart loads. Kit was the name of our old pony, and she seemed to know as soon as the cart was empty; she needed no shouts of 'whoa gal'. She stopped as soon as the last forkful reached the top of the elevator. We children were forbidden to ride on the pole behind the pony, but my husband, Peter, when a boy of ten, sitting on the pole, caught his foot in the turning mechanism. His father, on top of the hay stack, hearing him shout, called whoa to the horse, who stopped immediately, so averting a serious accident.

The hay, once stacked, filled the yard with its sweet scent of mown grass and flowers. Then, during the winter, when the hay was needed, it was fed to the stabled cows and horses. To get the hay out from the tightly packed stack the hay knife was sharpened with a whetstone to a razor sharpness. Trusses of hay carted out of the stack always reminded me of Mother carving slices off her good plum cake. The smell of that newly-opened stack on those cold winter days brought back memories of summer and the waving grasses filled with flowers. How the animals enjoyed it, and should any escape from stable or cowshed, they made straight for the haystack.

We were not supposed to climb on to the haystack or play on the hay in the hay barn. Needless to say, we did, and would curl up on a nest of hay, with sunbeams dancing with dust motes creeping through cracks in the dark old barn, and dream our dreams, usually with a puppy or kitten for company, until we were called for our meal, or to run some errand. Quite often, if we thought it meant company and a wash and change of clothing to make us, as Mother stated, 'respectable and less like gypsies', we dug ourselves deeper into the hay and remained hidden.

The hay barn was a lovely old place, low-windowed with old beams;

bits of old leather harness hung on the walls and in the loft above, which one entered by climbing very rickety steps, let into the side of the barn. The loft was dark, the only light coming in from slits in the wall, a marvellous place to hide. You could see into the yard, but no one could see you looking out. The floor was of wooden planks, and in some places quite rotten. More old bits of harness, sacks and old implements were here. One side was open and looked down into the chaff house. Our greatest thrill, and a game we never tired of, was to throw ourselves backward or forward, and somersault into the deep chaff a few feet below. Needless to say we were not popular when we undressed for bed, and chaff spilled from our hair, clothes and shoes.

On the other side of the hay barn was the round house, usually filled with farm implements, ploughs, seed drills and suchlike. I loved that old building and spent many happy hours there, but without realising its historic importance. It was a horse-engine house, and could have been Bedfordshire's only surviving example, according to Terence Paul Smith, who was invited by K Fadden of the Ampthill and District Archaeological Society to record the building. The horse-engine house was built against the side of a low barn, once a threshing barn, where the corn would be threshed from the stalks with flails. The walling of the round house was of coursed, dressed ironstone, which would have been found locally. There were four large openings with limestone slabs for sills and there was a large opening for use as a doorway. The roof was covered with Welsh slates[1]. Many's the time I slid down that roof with dire results to strong navy knickers.

*Horse engine house at Priestley Manor Farm – drawn by Miss B Sewell*
*(by kind permission of Kevan Fadden)*

---

[1]   A full description can be found in 'A horse engine house at Priestley Farm, Flitwick', by Terence Paul Smith. Bedfordshire Archaeological Journal, Vol. 10, 1975, page 77.

These houses were built some time in the eighteenth century to contain a threshing machine worked by two or more horses. They probably took over from the original method of threshing by hand, with a flail, on the granary floor. Alas, in 1972 the engine house was badly damaged by fire and later demolished. A sad ending to the old building of so many memories.

My days at Priestley were peopled with ghosts from bygone days. I felt as one with those who had used those buildings long before I knew them, and was never afraid in their musky darkness. There were always animals moving around in the yard or byre; hens and cats appeared around every corner. Perhaps it was my imagination that sometimes caught a glimpse of a cowled monk or smocked shepherd. But I knew them all! They were my friendly people of the shadows.

## Harvest

Along the edge of the orchard grew a few old plum trees, and yellow-gages which, when ripe, would split and the juice, oozing honey-sweet from those cracked gages, is beyond description. We searched the grass beneath for any fallen fruit which the wasps had not devoured, and out mouths and hands became cloyed with juice mingled with dirt. Scoldings were ignored. We knew the plum harvest was short. About this time Father would announce the corn ready for harvesting. I could hardly wait for morning to come and was in the stable at the first light watching the horses being groomed and harnessed ready to pull the binder into the field, and start the reaping as soon as the sun had dried out the stalks of standing corn. A pathway round was first mown with scythes – cowman Tom Parker being one of the men good with a scythe – to save the horses trampling the corn. All being ready, off would go the rattling binder with flails flying. The first time round, the horses would be a bit fresh and have to be on a tight rein. The golden corn was bent by the revolving flails on to the sharp knives. A conveyor belt of canvas carried the cut corn into the mechanism which tied the corn into bundles with binder twine, and threw the sheaves out on to one side. Quite often the knotting mechanism would jam and the binder would be brought to a jolting halt while the troubles were sorted out.

There would be two, three, or sometimes four, horses to pull the binder, with a spare team tethered in the shade. With a team of two horses there would be one man on the binder to control machine and horses. With more than two horses often a boy would ride on the 'for-est' (leading horse), to guide it. The days were long and weary for both men and horses, but as the standing corn became less and less with just a patch standing, all the men from the farm, and boys from the nearby village

17

who could get there, would gather round with sticks and dogs. As the frightened rabbits rushed out, they were quickly disposed of and in many cottages there would be a succulent rabbit supper.

*Horses pulling the binder cutting a field of wheat. This picture was taken in 1921 at Thrupp End, Lidlington, the farm where Peter, my husband, was born.*

My father and brother were both good shots and would be there with guns. I hated carrying home the still warm dead rabbits (made easier for carrying, with one hind leg pushed through a slit made in the other), but thus laden I made my way home, the freshly-cut stubble poking into my sandalled feet making my feet sore, and the poor dead rabbits banging against my knees. Eventually, I decided to be missing at future 'last cut' rounds.

The sheaves lying on the stubble would be put into shocks, a group of six or eight sheaves, heads together propping one another up, so that the wind and sun could dry them out. This was done by a gang of men who seemed to leisurely walk round the field with sheaves under sun-tanned arms, leaving the shocks in long straight rows. It certainly was not as easy as it looked, especially when the sheaves were well-sprinkled with thistles.

With the weather fine, the corn would soon be ready to cart to the stack yard, though with oats Father always reckoned that 'Church bells should ring over the standing "shocks" three times'. The carts would be made ready with extra 'copse' (wooden frames) fitted to make a long loading body for the sheaves. The empty cart was taken to the corn field, and one or two men would pitch the sheaves of corn on to the waiting cart on which stood the man whose job it was to build a load of slippery sheaves, which would not slide off on the journey from field to stack yard. My job was to lead the horse from shock to shock called out to the man perched above, 'O'g' before we moved off. O'g was the name given to the one who led the horses and called to the man loading. Woe betide the one who was O'g, should the horse move before the call was made. It was many years after that I realised it was a shortening of 'Hold Ye'!

When the cart was loaded and roped securely, the horse was handed over to the driver of the waiting empty cart and the full cart taken back to the stack yard, where the men who were to build the stack were waiting. A base would have been prepared for the stack, consisting of dry bundles of brushwood. One man would be in charge of building the corn stacks; the other men would throw him the sheaves. One man, on the cart to unload, would take up a sheaf on his two-pronged fork, and throw it to another man on the stack, who passed it on to the builder of the stack. A great pride was taken in building the stack, and during its completion the man building would slide down from above and, with a practised eye, go round the stack, beating the ends of the sheaves until they became even. Sometimes things might go astray, or a younger man asked to try his hand, with the result that a stout pole was needed to prop up one side of the stack, and there it stood, a disgrace to the poor man, until the thrashing machine came to thrash out the leaning stack.

Harvest time was tiring, thirsty work, for all taking part, but there was a sense of fulfilment and pride as the strong sinewy brown arms of the men effortlessly pitched up those golden sheaves on to the top of the laden wagons. The air would be full of the jingle of the harness as the patient horses shook flies from their ears and their muscles would ripple under their sweat-smeared coats, as they threw their great shoulders into their collars and pulled the wagons from field to stack yard. The sound of voices could be heard as the men called to one another, and the quiet companionship of men and beast was apparent as they rested in the shade and ate the meal their wives had packed early that morning, which was sent from the farm in the empty cart, or drank their cold tea. The horses would be unhitched from the wagons at midday, given water to drink and put into the cool stables for an hour. Their bridles would be taken off, but the rest of the harness left on ready for the next session.

There was so much movement and colour to the old harvest scene, now taken over by the combine harvester with tractor and trailer. Gone is the poetry of the man pitching sheaves of golden corn, and the slow gentle plodding shire horse. But gone also are the aching limbs and muscles, and collar-sore shoulders.

One of the things we loved to do, if we did not ride in the empty carts (we were not allowed to ride back on the loaded carts. Mother had a word with the men, and when Mother spoke…!), was to swing on the unused knotted ropes slung beneath the copse, quite often falling flat on our backs in the dust. Sometimes we were trusted to drive the empty carts to the field, and always we would manoeuvre the cart under the yellow-gages, should the field lie in that direction. Bringing back the laden cart was not quite so easy. The way to the stack yard was through a gate and down a slope (today that slope is hardly there). The old horses knew their job. I held the end of the lead rope, shut my eyes (making sure my feet were not in the way of their great hoofs) and they led me though and down to the stack yard.

## Horses

Horses were my dearest friends. They carried me on their broad backs, put down their heads so that I could push on their collars, and stood patiently as I swung on it to turn it round. They looked kindly on me as I put on their blinkered bridle and pushed their forelocks out of their eyes. I sat in their mangers, and shared my secrets and sweets with them. All I ever wanted to do was to be with them. Any job I could do with a horse or pony, I was more than willing to do.

I remember two plough teams in the stables with several other horses to make up odd pairs, but Boxer and Prince, Daisy and Blossom were the main ones. Joe Walton ploughed with Boxer and Prince, and Ted Rolph with Daisy and Blossom. Daisy was a Suffolk Punch and walked much quicker than Blossom, so had to be reined back. A rope rein, called a 'Chap Rein' was attached to the bridle bit and tied on to the chain of the slower horse, thus keeping their heads level. Ploughing was a great skill. To plough a straight furrow at the right depth, keeping an even ridge on some of the stoney ground of Priestley was not easy.

The horses hardly needed guiding with the long lines, and quite often only one line attached to the bridle bit was used. The ploughman used his voice, and with a flick of an ear the horse would come on round, go on! who back! and know when to turn on the head-land, stepping sideways, jostling each other, flank by flank, they put their feet in the furrow and ridge ready for the return bout, the ploughman swinging on the handles, often sitting on them to lift and bring the plough-share round. Ploughing was a lonely job, just the acres of land to be ploughed, the horses and the birds following the plough. The horses would have a few minutes' rest at the end of each bout, (once up and down the field) and their working day usually finished at three o'clock in the afternoon. They were then unhitched from the plough, and the lines wound up and hung on the brass hames (pointed metal pieces of harness fitted to the collar), together with the ploughman's spare jacket and lunch bag. He would then hoist himself on the broad back of one of his team, and, sitting sideways, make way for home.

I would plod silently behind Joe Walton at plough for most of the afternoon, in the hope that he would lift me up on to Boxer's back, and I would ride home in sheer ecstasy. I can remember the feel of the old horse's sweaty lumbering body against my bare legs, as he carried me gently into the yard, where he put his great head into the trough and drank deeply of the cool water.

The horses were then taken into the low stables, unharnessed, fed, and brushed over. The horsekeeper went home to tea, returning later to bed the horses down with straw, give another feed of corn and hay, and 'set fair' for the night.

I would look in and see the lamplight shining on the straw and hear the steady 'munch, munch' as they pulled at their hay. They lifted their heads to look at me as I ran in at the doorway. The rope attached one end to their halters and the other end through a ring in the manger to a wooden block, would pull the block up to the manger with a clonk. They stared with wise old eyes and soon resumed their chumping of corn. The lantern was blown out, stable door closed and, apart from a shod hoof striking the cobbles and the rattle of the manger block, all was quiet. There is an entry in one of my Father's books, *viz*: 19 May 1943, 'Boxer died at work'. How sad we were at his death, so often had he carried me on his broad back. These horses were like members of our family, and we were always upset when at last their long lives came to an end.

## Other Farm Work

Muck carting; another job on the farm which was often done when the weather was frosty. The yards had usually been cleared of dung after the cattle had been turned out, and the dung carted to a large heap on the edge of a field. But larger heaps of strawy manure, thrown out of the cowhouse and stable, accumulated, and this had to be carted away. The muck-heap at the edge of the field had matured to a nice thick consistency, and this was loaded into the carts with four-tyned muck forks. This was then put on to the field in heaps, and the men would spread it evenly over the fields, ready to be ploughed in. A good healthy smell when out in the open, but indoors by the fire, one's clothes began to give off a far from pleasant odour, which called for instant banishment from the kitchen.

The sheep on the farm were mostly in pens of hurdles, either in the fields of turnips or amongst the brussel stalks, after the picking of the sprouts. The pens would be made with an extra one for the sheep to be moved into when one pen of stalks or turnips had been eaten clean. A double lot was made for the weekend, and so the sheep were moved over the fields. Will Peat was shepherd on the farm when Father first went to

Priestley. His son, Stanley, tells of his father's work with the sheep... 'I remember one year the Holly Hedge field was full of turnips on which my Dad penned the sheep, very interesting changing the pens every day. Dad had a very strong sheep dog; it would carry the stakes for him to hold up the hurdles. I remember one week sometime during the First World War, when I looked after some sheep on the bean stubble, my wage was 3s.6d. That was in my school holiday. That money went to a clockmender, to have a grandmother clock mended. His name was Mr Wilcox from Ampthill, and he charged 3s. for the four journeys'... There were sheep troughs on wheels which were filled with water, and feed for the lambing ewes. At lambing time the hurdles were thatched and straw bales put into position to give shelter to the newly-born lambs. Often there were weak or orphan lambs, and these were wrapped in flannel and put in the 'low' oven of the old kitchen range, where Mother's care would more often than not make them strong again. The orphan lambs were fed with an old beer bottle, to which was attached a special long-pointed teat made of thick rubber. We would sit by the fire with a woolly body under one arm thrusting the teat into its mouth, tipping the bottle so that the milk ran down into its little throat. They soon learnt how to suck and stand splay-legged on the old rag rug before the kitchen range, with tails wagging in ecstasy, milk dribbling down their chins, soon emptying the bottle.

The sheep were shorn at the end of May. A hand-turned shearing machine was used, and the woolly sheep soon became gaunt, and so unfamiliar that at first bewildered mothers were unrecognised by their lambs. Quite often the weather turned cold, and proved how wrong is the old saying ... 'He Tempers the Wind to the Shorne Lamb' (*Laurence Sterne, 1713–1768*). God doesn't always temper the winds, nor do you shear lambs!

## Winter on the Farm

Winter began for us when we were buttoned into thick underclothes, with scarves crossed over our chests and pinned at the back. We were clamped in with no escape, or so Mother thought. Usually we wriggled out of a few layers during the day, and woebetide if there was the sight of a sniffle. Out would come the camphorated oil and we were well rubbed. We must have frightened off, or struck dead, any lurking germs that dared to come near.

November the fifth was a great day for us. Rubbish had been collected over the last months and a huge bonfire made in Long Field, well away from the stack yard. Old rubber tyres were added (from Billingtons Garage). All day, if not at school, we had been busy making the guy, a

22

turnip from the clamp for a head and any old clothes we could scrounge. Nightfall could not come quickly enough, and then we all trooped to the bonfire. A great blaze shot up, Catherine Wheels whirled and shed sparks, or fell dejectedly from their pins! Rockets shot from bottles and the sky shone with multi-coloured stars. Wretched boys let off Jumping Jacks and Thunder-Flashes, which frightened the life out of nervous little girls waving sparklers in their gloved hands. Best of all, I loved the Golden Rain, and even now, in late autumn when the golden beech leaves tumble down, I see again that blazing bonfire and the fireworks shooting heavenwards and falling in a golden shower.

During the winter, cattle and horses would be brought into yards and stable, and there would be extra work night and morning, mucking out cowsheds and stables early in the morning, and bedding down with clean straw in the evening. Hay and fodder had to be prepared, mangers filled, water buckets topped up, and mangels taken from the clump, chopped and thrown to sheep. The cart horses often had a mangel put into their manger. They loved to crunch on them, and the old horsekeeper said it kept their gums healthy. On very wet days the harness would be taken down and oiled, and looked over for repairs. Sacks had to be sorted through and repaired, and placed into their respective heaps, potato sacks, corn sacks, chaff sacks; cart wheels were greased, barrows mended and barns tidied.

Hard frost and deep snow added to our excitement, but not to that of the men. Frozen pipes and water troughs had to be thawed before thirsty stock could drink, or the milking start. Hurdles were frozen into the ground, making it almost impossible to re-pen the sheep; and handling frozen mangels with chillblained hands in a biting east wind is sheer agony.

The stables and cow byres were warm with the heat of the animals, and milking by hand with one's face pressed into the cow's warm flank, with milk flowing freely from a warm udder, was almost bliss, until the cow swung her tail and landed a stinging slap across the face, or kicked out and put her foot in a full pail of milk, sending it flying.

Best of all were the chat or pig potatoes (small potatoes) cooked in an old boiler outside the pig sties. The rusty iron boiler would be filled with cold water and potatoes, and a fire lit underneath to boil the water and cook the potatoes. When they were cold they were shovelled out, mixed with swill (pig meal, water or milk) and fed to the pigs. As soon as the potatoes were cooked, we would hook out some whole ones with a sharpened stick and eat them. They were delicious. I think my peck of dirt has been trebled long ago.

The ponds froze over and we slid and skated on them, fell through the thin ice around the edges, ran home grizzling with wet cold feet and fingers, were scolded, given hot sweet orange juice and were away to the pond again.

A great treat in a very severe winter was to be allowed to skate or slide on the lake in the park of Flitwick Manor. Miss Brooks, and later Colonel and Mrs Lyall, would allow the people of Flitwick access to the lake, one end of which was kept free of ice for swans and water fowl to swim around in. How large that lake seemed to me, and I remember one very frosty moonlit evening, the lake peopled with skaters gliding along and others watching on the bank, I wanted to stay forever but knew I must make my way home, so I ran across the moonlit field to Priestley. That must have been the last time we skated there before the 1939 war started.

*An up-to-date picture of the park and lake at Flitwick Manor, where we were allowed to skate during hard frosty weather before World War Two. (by kind permission of Mr and Mrs E Billington)*

Christmas at Priestley was always something special, starting in November when, in the large kitchen with the fire in the kitchen range glowing red and the oil lamp lit, Mother and I would sit at the scrubbed kitchen table, and with a damp cloth between us would stone the dark plump raisins, wiping our sticky fingers on the cloth, and putting the stones into a bowl of warm water. The stoned raisins were placed in a blue ringed bowl ready for the making of the Christmas puddings. I still use Mother's old recipe, and the puddings turn out rich and dark. All the family stirred the pudding and as a small child my wish was always the same every year – a pony.

Threepenny pieces were wrapped in greaseproof paper (so that we did not swallow them) and added to the pudding mixture, which was divided into china pudding basins, the top covered with greaseproof paper, a snow-white cloth tied into rabbits' ears (i.e. the ends brought to the middle and tied), and string tied tightly around the basin and cloth. The basins were then placed into the boiling water in the copper, which had been lined with an old towel in the bottom, and cooked for twelve hours. Kettles of water were kept boiling on the kitchen range to keep the copper full to half way up the basins. After twelve hours they were taken out and laid on their sides until the basins and puddings were cold. They then had clean white cloths put on and were stored on the top of the kitchen dresser. A row of Christmas puddings stood there from one year to the next. Often the previous year's pudding would be eaten on Christmas Day with brandy butter, brandy sauce and thick cream. No one worried about calories. In fact, I am sure we had never heard of the word!

There would be roast turkey with all the trimmings, carved by Father at the head of the table, with potatoes and brussels sprouts, home grown of course. No other brussels sprouts seemed to taste as good as Bedfordshire grown sprouts. Before our meal, Father would thank God, and Mother, for our good dinner.

Very early on Christmas morning we would wake and beg for a candle. Already we had felt the bolster case hung at the foot of the bed to make sure Father Christmas had called. We were lucky, it was full of parcels of all shapes and sizes. No longer could we wait for morning light and, at last, a candle was lit and Christmas had come.

One Christmas morning long ago, very early, my brother, Richard, rushed into my room begging me to 'look outside'. I flew to the window thinking at last I should see Father Christmas and his reindeer. But no, it was out on the landing I had to look, and there in all its spotted glory stood a grey dappled rocking horse, with a real mane and tail, and flaring nostrils and a red saddle and bridle. How I loved that rocking horse, and what imaginary journeys we took together.

The dining room was decorated each year with the same old paper decorations. They came to Wiltshire with me, but a few years ago they simply fell to pieces. A large paper bell of red, green and blue hung above the door and swung round and round in the draught. A decorated Christmas tree stood in the corner and the firelight reflected in the silver balls. Sugar mice and a sugar pig were always on the tree.

Mother, when a little girl living on a remote farm in Hertfordshire, was given a few pennies at Christmas. She would walk several miles to a little shop where she would choose and purchase a sugar pig. That sugar pig was her only Christmas treat.

Sometimes there would be relations staying at Christmas and in the evening, after supper of cold turkey, pickles, mincepies, cheese, etc., the big old table was cleared, drinks poured out, and young and old gathered together around the table to play 'tip it'. 'Tip it' is played with two teams, one team each side of the table, each team with a captain. One team starts with both hands hidden under the table, where a small coin is passed from hand to hand. Eventually the captain calls 'hup' and all hands firmly clenched are placed on the top of the table. One member of the opposite team has to guess in which hand the coin was hidden. He will ask certain people to take their hands off the table until he comes to the hand he thinks holds the coin. Then, he yells 'tip it', striking the hand. If he has chosen correctly his team then takes the coin, and continues the game. Later on during the evening there would be card games, Nap, Rummy or Newmarket, whilst younger children curled up on the hearth rug and played Donkey, Old Maid, Draw the Well Dry, and Snap. Most of all I remember Christmas morning before breakfast. Father would play on the old wind-up gramaphone, the record of a choir singing 'Oh Come All Ye Faithful'.

The New Year came in quietly at Priestley. If awake we would stand shivering outside to listen for the sound of church bells ringing in the New Year, then stumbled sleepily back to our beds. Routine work on the farm continued as before; sheep, cattle and horses always need food and water.

## Threshing

The day the threshing machine arrived at Priestley was one of the highlights of our lives. I could never understand Father's attitude towards that gorgeous panting monster of a machine. How could he be so pleased to see its departure?[1] When we knew the day of its coming, we would spend hours perched on top of the five-barred gate half way along the stony road to watch for the first signs of smoke as it passed the holly hedge. The threshing engine puffed along, its large iron wheels grating and pounding the road. Behind the engine was attached the threshing drum and chaff cutter. On top of the drum would be the bikes, coats and lunch bags of those connected with the threshing outfit. The captain of the wonderful 'craft' was Herbert Robinson, and pipe in mouth, kerchief at his neck, he swung the wheel with dexterity, which guided his engine, chunting though difficult narrow farm gates, backing engine and drum with precision by the stack which was to be threshed. The black engine huffed and puffed, the wheel turned, swung by strong arms, and at last all

---

[1] The threshing tackle, as it was called, came from Mr Woodlands of Ridgmont.

was in position. Oil can and rags were then produced, pistons and moving parts oiled and cleaned, the fire box damped down, and with gentle hissing sobs the engine settled down for the night. The men left for home on their bikes and we stood and admired from a distance the wonderous beast. It was left ready to begin work in the morning.[1]

Prior to the threshing engine's coming, a horse and cart had been despatched to Flitwick Station for a load of steam coal, which was dumped in the rick yard and white paint splashed on it less some poor soul was tempted to burn it on their fire. Old Taffy, one of the horses used only for light work, as he was broken-winded, would be harnessed and put to the water cart, which was filled from the brook which ran through the meadow. The full water cart was placed near the threshing engine with a pipe from its boiler entering the top of the cart. Each day the cart was refilled for the thirsty engine.

*Group of corn threshers near Flitton, with Tommy Anderson (my Brother Richard's father-in-law) in charge of the machine.*
*(By kind permission of Bedfordshire County Record Office – PU 373/1973).*

---

[1] Some years ago there had been much rain, and the threshing tackle got set in the soft ground of the stack yard. A very strong horse by the name of Duke was brought out from the stable to help pull the tackle free from the mud. I remember Duke, a massive dark bay horse. I was told he was an ex-Army horse released from the Army after the 1914–18 war. How those poor animals must have suffered during that terrible time; pulling heavy machinery through deep mud would have been no new experience for him.

Early next morning threshing would begin. The fire box of the engine was raked out and glowing embers coaxed into flame and made into a furnace with the coal. Steam up. The great flywheel began to turn and the belt from the flywheel to a smaller wheel on the drum began to flop and turn the drum, which rumbled hungrily, and the men on the stack, which had already been stripped of its thatch, stuck their two-pronged forks into the sheaves, throwing them to the man standing on top of the drum. He caught them, cut the binder twine with his sharp knife (known as a shut knife), and dropped the loosened sheaf into the maw of the greedy drum. Thick hessian corn sacks were hung at one end of the drum, down whose shutes the corn peppered against your palms like shot, a marvellous feeling. When the bags were full, the man in charge of them quickly took them off, first pulling over a small lever to cut off the chute of corn while another sack was fixed. The full bag was tied with hessian string, put on to a sack barrow and wheeled to a waiting cart, or barn, where it was to be stored. The sacks of corn weighted two hundredweight each, so the strongest men on the farm had the handling of the corn sacks.

From the end of the drum came the straw, which was either built into a stack for winter use, or put through the chaff cutter to come out all chopped up into golden flakes, which were to be mixed with animal feed for the winter, the chaff adding bulk to their feed and helping their digestion.

At Priestley, the chaff house being so near to the stacks in the stack yard, the chaff was blown into the chaff house through long tubes, otherwise it would have to be carried there in large chaff sacks.

The dirtiest job of all was carrying the cavings from the machine. Cavings came from the drum down a separate chute to the straw, and were the husks and rubbish from the sheaves of corn. This was also very dusty, and a job no one liked doing. The cavings were either burnt or thrown to the pigs in their paddock. They received them with grunts of delight and much wiggling of tails, rolling about and rootling in them.

As the stack neared the bottom , the men had further to throw up the sheaves on to the drum, and out of the base ran scores of mice and rats. All the cats on the farm were aware of this and waited with tails flicking. The terrier dogs (we always had one or two about the farm) yelped and barked with eager anticipation. We were all armed with sticks and joined in the chase. There was such a combined attack that few vermin escaped. But there would always be a wise old mother cat (usually tortoise-shell) who waited quietly in the background and caught the one who thought he had got away.

When all the stacks had been threshed, the threshing drum equipment would be packed up, hitched to the engine and away it would chuff to another farm, leaving behind a pile of cinders, heaps of dusty straw and some very sad children and well-filled cats.

The stacks of straw would be made safe from winter gales, the rick yard tidied up, the loose and dusty straw burnt, and the farm work was back to routine.

## Blacksmith

'How far from then forethought of, all thy more
      boisterous years
When thou at the randome grim forge, powerful
      amidst peers,
Didst fettle for the great grey dray horse
      his bright and battering sandle!'
*From Felix Randal by Gerard Manley Hopkins*

For all farms the local blacksmith was a necessity, not only for the shoeing of horses, but to repair farm machinery, ploughs, harrows or any parts that were made of iron. Iron fencing was often used round farm gardens and church yard; this would be made in the forge by the local blacksmith. During the Second World War many of these railing were removed and turned into bomb casings, etc. The blacksmith's forge at Flitwick had stood for several centuries on the green by the village pond at Hornes End. This pond was, alas, filled in long ago. The old Fir Tree inn stood nearby, in front of which grew a tall fir tree from which the inn got its name. At the back of the forge was a piece of garden land which, at certain times of the years, was full of frogs. On one side of the forge was the village school; on the opposite side of the road lay the wheelwright's workshop.

There is a reference to the forge as early as 1671, when a George Swayre was the Flitwick blacksmith. The 1881 census shows us that William Cain, aged fifty-nine, and his son Thomas Cain, fifteen, were blacksmiths at Flitwick. In April 1885 a William Carr, son of a shepherd from Beckerings Park, Steppingley, was apprenticed to James Denton, blacksmith at Flitwick. The indentures say that 'James Denton shall teach and instruct the art of blacksmith to Wm. Carr for a term of four and a half yrs, and provide meat, drink and lodgings for one shilling per week'. After his apprenticeship Mr Wm. Carr left Flitwick to work at Ampthill and then Surrey, returning to Flitwick when the forge became vacant. There he was blacksmith with his son Roland. Roland retired in 1964, and sadly the forge was closed.[1]

---

[1] I am indebted to the late Mrs B Carr and the late Miss D Carr for information on Wm. R Carr, Blacksmith, and for the Christmas Card showing Flitwick Blacksmith's forge.

*Flitwick, Bedfordshire.*

*A Greetings Card scene of Flitwick forge, with the school in the background, painted by Sylvester Stannard.*

How well I remember, as a child, being taken to the forge and that very same William Carr lifting me up in his strong arms and holding me over the glowing fire. It must have been some kind of initiation for me because, as I grew up, I spent so many happy hours in that old forge, where I was allowed to blow the fire with the bellows. This was a great honour, because the bellows had to be pumped at a slow steady speed to get the embers to the correct heat: no sudden speed and spurting of flames, otherwise the iron being heated would be spoilt.

Blacksmiths measure mostly with their eye, and use a piece of chalk to mark off their bar of iron, seldom needing to measure again. When making shoes for any size horse or pony, it always remained a mystery to me how they could tell what size the piece of iron had to be that they heated, hammered, and heated again; then, glowing hot, the iron, now horse-shoe shape, carried with pincers, would be held, sizzling, against the horse's hoof, which had already been neatly pared down with a curved sharp knife (toeing or drawing knife), and long-handled pincers. A strong, never to be forgotten, acrid smell of scorching hoof and hair filled the forge and wafted on the air through the open door. The shoe was then taken back to the fire, heated again, placed on an anvil, the clenches knocked in, and nail holes punched in with hammer and pritchel (a punch-like tool). The blacksmith's hammer rang out as iron struck iron and clanged on the anvil. As a drummer beats rhythm on his drums, so is the rhythm of the blacksmith's hammer on his anvil, as he fashions heated iron into horse shoes.

When finished, the shoes were plunged, sizzling into a tank of rusty-looking water, which stood near the fire. The set of shoes was then nailed on to the horse's hoofs quickly and firmly, the clenches hammered down, and ends of nails rasped off: a quick rasp round the end of hoof and shoe, a lick of an oily brush kept in a jar of oil specially for this purpose, and the horse was ready for the road.

Whilst the horse is being shod, its hoof rests on an iron tripod, or on the blacksmith's leather-aproned knee. Some horses do not stand quietly to be shod and made the shoeing hard mauling work. Others stand quietly, lifting their hooves when bidden to do so. Quite often they, just for the 'hell' of it, will put all their weight on the leg the smith is holding up, causing him to shout, 'Stand up you old b.....'. The horse, with a surprised look, as if to say, 'What, me? I'm not doing anything wrong', quickly shifts its weight on to its own three legs. They will often slyly nibble away at the blacksmith's bent back, causing a few more choice words!

I used to spend many hours with our farm horses at the Flitwick Blacksmith's; arriving early in the morning, riding from the farm on their bare backs and, though forbidden to do so by Father, I would urge them into a canter as we crossed the fields. To feel the power of those great bodies pounding along was marvellous. I now know how those knights in shining armour must have felt as they galloped into the lists to joust. Only for me it was so much better. I was free of any heavy equipment, clad in a jumper and pair of shorts or slacks, and for my steed a blinkered bridle and leather rein. Over the fields of Priestley we sped, their great hooves flinging up clods of earth, me clinging to their thick flowing manes. I am sure the exhilaration was as great as that of Sir David de Flitwick (Knight) who, in 1308, trotted forth to take part in a mounted tournament at Dunstable.[1]

A blacksmith's forge was a meeting place in a village: many a story is told there and advice sought. The blacksmith usually knows for whom the passing bell is being tolled, (during my childhood it was still used), whether so-and-so's baby is a boy or girl, whose harvest is ready, what crops are good or bad, who has been picked for the village

---

[1]  J Godber, 'History of Bedfordshire', p.72

cricket/football team, the latest world news, and even where Mrs —
purchased her new hat for the church fête. A blacksmith knows all about
a horse's foot and bones of the legs, so his advice is often sought before
that of a Vet, should a horse become lame. Also, many was the time one
of my homework mathematical problems was worked out round that old
forge fire. My ponies loved to stand with their heads over the half door of
the blacksmith's forge, as I chatted away, and my dog, Zipp, chewed with
relish a rind of twisted hoof thrown to her.

One day, Mother, resplendent in her 'Queen Mary' toque of navy silk,
drove Beauty, harnessed to the Governess Cart, to collect some shopping
at Flitwick. Suddenly, instead of proceeding sedately along the road, she
found herself outside the forge. Beauty's head already hanging over the
door ready for a long rest and chat. To Mother's great embarrassment she
had to be led back on to the road where, to her chagrin, Rol Carr asked
her for the winner of the forthcoming big race.

Mother loved her little gamble of 6d each way on the big flat races, but
thought it was a deep secret to all. I can imagine it was with much
tut-tutting that Beauty was shaken into a smart trot away into the village.

Sadly there are no longer working horses on the farms to be taken
along to the forge; riding ponies and horses are often shod in their home
stables by a blacksmith who has made the shoes beforehand, which are
then nailed on to the hoof cold. I remember being told by old Mr William
Carr, 'A cold blacksmith will freeze in hell'.

Times have changed.

## The Fires

Buildings of any kind on fire are a frightening sight. Farm fires down
through the ages have been no exception. Stables, cowsheds, barns, corn
and haystacks as well as farm houses and farm cottages have been at risk.
During the Farm workers' riots, the firing of stacks and machinery was
one of the terrors the farmers had to watch out for. All animals will panic
at the sight and sound of fire, and it takes a lot of courage to get horses
out of a burning stable. Often the horse if too terrified to move and has to
be blindfolded to get it through the flames.

A spark from the threshing engine could start off a fire in thatched
cottages as it chuffed by, so great care was taken in the actual stack yard
when the engine was installed for threshing.

Then there was the overheating of a newly-built hay stack to watch for.
Each morning a long thin rod of iron, about ten to twelve feet with a ring
handle, was inserted from first one side of the stack then the other, the rod
reaching the centre, and was left in the stack for some hours and then
withdrawn and tested by hand to see how hot the stack was. One morning

the rod came out almost red hot. The Fire Brigade was summoned at once, and all hands formed a human chain to pass buckets of water to the burning stack. Down the stony road rushed the fire engine, followed by the local bobby (policeman) on his bike and, following hard behind him, the young men of the village who had means of transport. Carefully the top of the stack was removed and, with bated breath, we prayed it would not explode into flames. The burning part of the haystack was uncovered and dowsed with water and the air stank for several days with the acrid smell of burnt hay.

The reason for the overheating was because the hay had been stacked whilst there was too much moisture in the grass stalks, instead of leaving it longer to dry in the sun and wind. Once compressed into a stack, the heat built up, causing combustion. What was left of the stack was then carted off to the muckheap and later ploughed into the land. On many farms the loss of a hay stack or stacks of corn would mean disaster, as the stacks were the main source of winter feed for the livestock. The haystack fire I remembered above was bad enough, but Priestley had had far worse fires.

In 1921, four years before I was born, a serious fire broke out in the stack yard at Priestley. We children were told of it many times to make us aware how careful we must be with matches and fire of any description. How worried Mother and Father must have been watching helplessly while the flames devoured the ricks. But, according to the report in the local newspaper, many friends gathered to help fight the fire and no livestock was lost. Here is a copy of that report:

### FLITWICK

A serious fire broke out on Tuesday, about 3pm at Priestley Farm, occupied by Mr W F Cole. It started from some unascertained cause, in a rick of unthreshed barley erected last harvest in the rick yard, a few yards behind the farm buildings. These buildings are brick-built, except the implement house, which is of timber and are the property of the Duke of Bedford. On either side of the rick mentioned were two other stacks of beans and linseed respectively and fanned by the wind, the flames reached, and involved, these and a wheat stack about 20 yards away. The Ampthill Fire Brigade arrived in about three-quarters of an hour, in charge of Captain E Foster, and water for the motor fire engine was drawn from the Flitt stream which runs within reach of the farm. Two of the buildings caught fire in the roof, one being the timber erection and another containing a store of chaff, but these were

33

saved. The four ricks were totally destroyed. Part of a rick of peastraw and a rick of hay were untouched.

Mr Cole and neighbouring farmers and their men worked strenuously to save any extension of the damage, which as it is will reach near to four figures, and which is covered by insurance.

Later, in 1972, twenty-five years after we had left Priestley, there was another fire which was thought to have been started by a tractor. It killed two calves and destroyed several buildings, including the lovely old Round House (Horse Engine House, mentioned earlier in this chapter).

This fire was reported in the *Ampthill News* in 1972. It is interesting to note the different styles of reporting.

### CALVES DIE AS FIRE FOLLOWS EXPLOSION...
#### (By Geoff Cox)

A row of barns was destroyed and two calves killed in a blaze which caused £7,000 worth of damage at Priestley Farm, Flitwick, on Monday.

It is believed that the fire started when a spark from a back-firing tractor set light to straw stored in one of the barns. The tractor's petrol tank then blew up. Firemen from Ampthill, Woburn, Kempston and Dunstable were called to fight the blaze which started in mid-afternoon. It took them nearly two hours to bring it under control.

### SPREAD

The tenancy of the Bedfordshire County Council farm is shared by Mr Eric Bonner and Mr Gilbert Little. Mr Little's father, Mr Frank Little, said, 'The fire spread along the barns and set light to some hay in a loft adjoining our calves. My son managed to save nine of the calves, but he could not get through the smoke and flames to the two that died.'

A £400 sprayer and other farm equipment was destroyed in the blaze, which cut off electricity. Mr Little was worried about milking his herd of 60 cows but managed to get an emergency generator working.

'All the farm buildings are very close together. If there had been a wind the farm house and all the animals nearby would have been in real danger.'

Mr Douglass Jeaves, fire prevention officer for the Dunstable area, said, 'A spark from a backfiring vehicle can easily set fire to straw. Machinery with combustion engines should not be garaged in farm buildings where straw is kept.'

A Dunstable police spokesman said, 'We are satisfied there are no suspicious circumstances.'

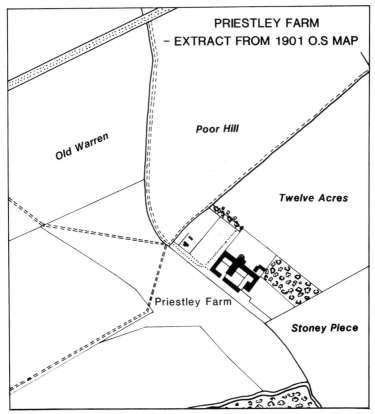

PRIESTLEY FARM
– EXTRACT FROM 1901 O.S MAP

Poor Hill

Old Warren

Twelve Acres

Priestley Farm

Stoney Piece

*Priestley Farmhouse and farm buildings, showing the round horse engine house, destroyed in fire, 1972. (Reproduced from the 1901 Ordnance Survey map.)*

During the Second World War, latish one autumn night, Father was returning by train from London when the air-raid warning sounded and the train halted along the track between Westoning and Flitwick station. All the lights in the carriages were out and there was the sound of enemy aircraft overhead. After a short while, Father peered cautiously out of the window and saw, to his horror, the fields of Priestley alight. Luckily it was just a stick of incendiary bombs which had been dropped on fields of stubble and soon burnt out.

Today we watch, after each harvest, the stubble fields blazing. The crimson flare lights the sky and no doubt there are many who think back, as I do, to those wartime nights when, with sinking hearts, we saw the glow lighting the sky from those devastated bombed towns and cities.

# Chapter 3

# Priestley Farmhouse

We do not exactly know what the houses were like in this part of England before the Roman invasion, except that they were made of rough hewn timber and other natural materials. During the centuries of Roman influence the better off farmers copied the styles and building materials of the townspeople and the occasional country villa had a mosaic floor, and

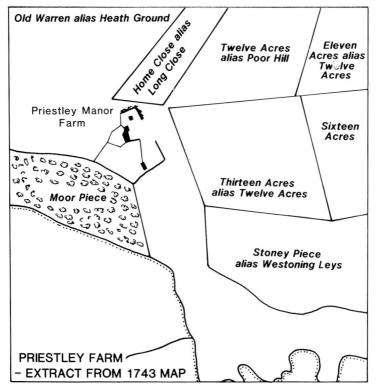

*Original house on site of current Gig House. (By kind permission of Mr J C Lyall and Bedfordshire County Record Office – LL4/1.)*

even central heating! However, during the early years of Saxon settlement the houses were once again very primitive. There were some improvements during the centuries leading up to the Norman Conquest but the thanes who were farming land at Priestley in 1066 would have lived in very simple houses.

Thorgils, the first Norman tenant, may have chosen to live at Priestley, in which case he would have started the development of what became a comfortable manor house. If, as suggested in *Flitwick – A Short History*,[1] Priestley Farm is the house which, in 1673, was recorded as having seven fireplaces, it was nearly as big as the manor house in Flitwick village, which had ten.

A map of 1743 shows the site of the old farm house, but on a map of 1807 only farm buildings are shown. Either the house was demolished or incorporated into the farm buildings. The absentee owners must have neglected the old manor house and let it fall into a dangerous condition. It is possible that the Duke of Bedford's steward had it taken down.

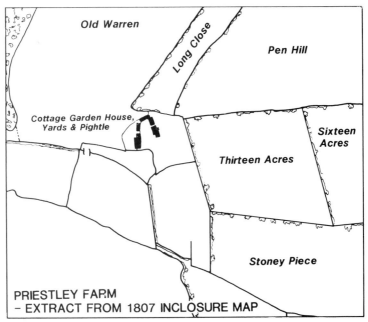

*Original house demolished. Current house built showing Horse Engine House on farm buildings. (By kind permission of Bedfordshire County Record Office – MA 68/1.)*

---

[1] 'Flitwick, A Short History', by Ampthill & District Archaeoligical & Local History Society, p.12, The 17th Century.

In 1787, Priestley Manor was sold to the Duke of Bedford. The present house, where I was born and lived until 1947, stands overlooking the meadows, woods and the River Flit, and was built during the brief reign of William IV, some time between 1830-40. It is of red brick, Georgian

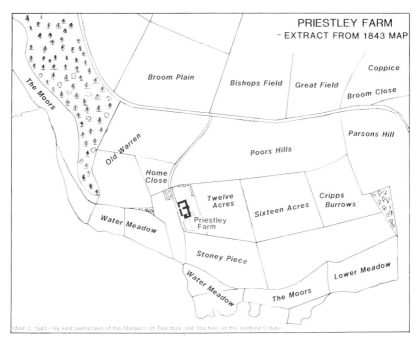

*Earliest map showing current farmhouse. (By kind permission of the Marquess of Tavistock and the Trustees of the Bedford Estate.)*

design, and the north wing was added a few years later. On the first floor, facing south, is a window painted out in black with white lines representing glazing bars. I am not sure if this was because of the window tax, which was abolished in 1851 (after the house was built), though it is more than likely this was done to give proportion to the Georgian front of the house. There is also another bricked-in window on the first floor facing north. The brick infill is of the same period as that of the house. This is obviously to keep the proportion of the building. The rooms within the house had blank walls where these blocked-in windows occurred.

At the same time as the house was built, in 1830-40, more farm buildings were added and the older buildings were incorporated into the new ones. The original old house at Priestley witnessed many changes. It watched while

-COPY OF-

-LEASE-

-OF-

PRIESTLEY FARM, FLITWICK.

THIS LEASE made the Fourteenth day of October One thousand
nine hundred and forty seven BETWEEN THE MOST NOBLE HASTINGS TWELFTH
DUKE OF BEDFORD (hereinafter called the Lessor which expression where
the context admits shall include the person or persons entitled to the
reversion of the property hereby demised expectant on the term hereby granted)
of the one part and the COUNTY COUNCIL OF THE ADMINISTRATIVE COUNTY OF
BEDFORD ( herein-after called the Lessees which expression where the
context admits shall include persons deriving title under them) of the
other part......................................................................

WITNESSETH in consideration of the rent hereinafter reserved
and of the Lessees' covenants hereinafter contained as follows:- ..........

1.          The Lessor hereby demises unto the Lessees ALL THAT house
two cottages buildings and Farm land called Priestley Farm situate in
the Parish of Flitwick in the County of Bedford and containing Two
hundred and twenty nine acres three roods twelve perches more or less
more particularly described in the Schedule hereto and delineated on
the plan annexed hereto and thereon edged pink and hereinafter referred
to as the demised property Except and Reserved unto the Lessor all timber
and timberlike trees pollards saplings tellers and underwood and all mines
ores and minerals surface stones beds of stone gravel brick earth clay
and sand and all waters and water courses with liberty to divert the
course thereof at pleasure and the concurrent use of the accustomed roads
and paths leading to any woods or other lands of the Lessor and with full
liberty of entrance for himself and those whom he may appoint with horses
carts engines machinery a nd implements to take possession of any land
and to do all things necessary to enable him to take the full benefit of
such exceptions and reservations paying to the Lessees reasonable
compensation for land taken and damage done or loss incurred and also full
liberty for the Lessor and others authorised by him to enter on the

*Copy of lease of Priestley Farm between the Twelfth Duke of Bedford
and Bedfordshire County Council, dated 14 October 1947.
(By kind permission of Bedfordshire County Record Office – AOS 23/4/2/1)*

of the said term and of such desire shall give to the other party at

least one year's previous notice in writing then at the expiration of

the said seventh or fourteenth year asthe case may be the term hereby

granted shall cease but without prejudice to the rights and remedies of the

Lessor for any arrears of rent or any breach of the Lessees' povenants...

IN WITNESS whereof the Lessor has hereunto set his hand and

seal and the Lessees have caused their Common Seal to be hereunto affixed

the day and year first above written...............................

----THE SCHEDULE above referred to-----

| No. on Plan | Names of fields &c. | Buildings & Orchard A R P | Arable A. R. P | Pasture A R P | Total A R P |
|---|---|---|---|---|---|
| 109 | Part of Poors Hill | | 20 0 15 | | |
| 110 | ditto | | 15 1 0 | | |
| 113 | Cripps Meadow | | 12 3 16 | | |
| 114 | Far Stony piece | | 18 2 20 | | |
| 116 | The Moors | | 14 1 20 | | |
| 117 | Near Stony piece | | 16 2 20 | • | |
| 118 | Sixteen acres | | 27 0 35 | | |
| 125 | Part of Old Warren | | | 10 1 5 | |
| 126 | ditto | | 18 0 18 | | |
| 127 | Water Meadow | | 10 2 20 | | |
| 129 | The Moors | | 11 2 26 | | |
| 130 | Clack Close | | | 9 0 25 | |
| 119) 120) | House, Homestead Garden, Orchard and belt | 3 3 12 | | | |
| 115 | Lower Meadow | | | 9 1 21 | |
| 122) 124) | Home Close and Water Meadow | | | 10 0 5 | |
| Pt. 82 | Parsons Hill | | 12 0 26 | | |
| | | 3 3 12 | 177 2 16 | 47 3 16 | 229 1 4 |
| 121 | COTTAGES (No 2 Priestley Farm ( (No.3 ditto | 2 8 | | | 2 8 |
| | | 4 1 20 | 177 2 16 | 47 3 16 | 229 3 12 |

Signed Sealed and Delivered by the above named )
The Most Noble Hastings Twelfth Duke of Bedford)      (Signed)    'Bedford'
in the presence of:-                             )

        (Signed)   E. Imogen Dix

              Crowholt, Woburn, Bletchley
              Secretary to his Grace the Duke of Bedford.

the neighbouring fields were ploughed up for corn and grassed over for sheep, only to be ploughed up once again as farmers experimented with different crops and farming methods. It stood through wars abroad and wars at home. It watched helplessly as the local people suffered such disasters as plague and other terrible diseases, fire, flood and famine. It was a silent witness to the harshness of life; where little girls were made to work from dawn to long after dusk and little boys were forced up chimneys.

The present house was built whilst there was deep unrest among the farm labourers (see Chapter 8), but it has stood proudly through Queen Victoria's sixty-three glorious years, followed by the reigns of Edward VII, George V, Edward VIII (although never crowned) and George VI, and still stands stalwartly today, in the reign of our Queen, Elizabeth II.

In 1947 Priestley Farm saw even more changes when it was leased to the Bedfordshire County Council by the Twelfth Duke of Bedford.

In December 1947, Fleet and Cave of Flitwick, Bedfordshire, put in a tender of £700.13s.9d., for adaptation of the Farm House.[1] Thereupon the house was divided into two dwellings.

*Priestley Farm Cottage after modernization in 1948.*
*(By kind permission of Betty Chambers.)*

The two farm cottages built by the Duke of Bedford in 1856 were extended and modernised in 1948, with further extension in 1969. In 1955 Bedfordshire County Council purchased Priestly Farm, and converted the two cottages into one home. The Priestley Farm House is still divided into two dwellings.

---

[1]    Bedfordshire County Record Office, AOC 23/4/1/1-18

## My Home
The very oldest part of the house, which we called the back rooms, and which no longer exist, consisted of two rooms, leading one from the other, over which was a room (or loft) which was entered by climbing wooden rungs let into the wall.

*Priestley Farm House, taken from the garden before Mother and Father went to live there in 1914. (I have been unable to trace the names of the two people in the picture.)*

The farthest room had a small, paned window overlooking the laurels in the garden. These laurels hid a very old privy (lavatory) where Mother used to set her broody hens on eggs. In this back room was a bin for chicken corn and dog biscuits, those big square slab ones, also shoe-cleaning materials, my saddles and bridles and other oddments, and plenty of spiders. In the first room there were big trays where Mother put her washing to soak, one for her whites and one for her coloureds. Boxes of Sunlight and Lifebuoy soap were kept in the airing cupboard in the scullery to go hard and so last longer. Bluebags and starch were also kept here together with black lead with brushes, and whitening stone. There were buckets for the pig swill. All leftovers went into these buckets, which were then mixed with meal and fed to the pig who lived in a sty in the hen-yard. Mother always had a house-pig and hens, which were her 'perks'. Some steps led up to a door leading into the hen-yard and over the door grew a sweet-scented rambling rose. Buckets of coal stood ready in this room, also wood for the fire, and quite often, if the cats had been lazy, one would come across a rat making a hasty retreat. It did not remain long once Mother knew of its presence. Sometimes my brother's ferrets would get loose and they seemed to find their way into the old room. I would quickly catch and return them to their quarters, before more trouble was made. On the wall hung the frying pans. These were of heavy metal, and were never washed, just wiped clean. No food ever stuck when cooked in them. What breakfasts came from those pans; freshly-gathered mushrooms, cooked with home-cured bacon, that was crisp, fried eggs from hens that wandered where they would, succulent liver and kidneys, and bread fried to a golden crispness, all served up on a blue patterned dish. My brother and I fought for the privilege of mopping up the juices with good crusty bread.

The large scullery, with its red-bricked floor, led from the back room. Here was a copper which was filled from a hand pump with soft rain water, - it smelt a bit high in summer, - an old brick bread-oven over a tunnel-like compartment, where the wood faggots for heating the oven were once kept, and a sink with cold water tap and hand pump. When electicity came to the farm in 1938, an electric pump was installed. Water was pumped up into tanks in the roof twice a day. There was also, at one time or another, an oil stove for cooking, then a calor gas stove, and, finally, an electric cooker. The coal range for most of the cooking was, however, in the kitchen. A long wide shelf ran along the back of the scullery, on which stood the large iron cooking pots, and above these was the square wooden shutter, which was opened to let out the steam on washing days. The window was above the sink, and double doors from the yard opened into the room. I remember riding my pony through the doors and round the scullery for a dare! I was not popular with Mother, or her helpers. I think the bricks had just been scrubbed. From the scullery a door led to the kitchen, which was a largish room with two windows, one overlooking the yard and the other the garden. Under this window grew a little creeping moss rose, in which, some years, a fly-catcher would build its nest

In the kitchen was the big old range, with its three ovens and glowing bars, and, along one wall, the dresser, on whose top reposed the Christmas puddings. Blue and white china rested along the other shelves. There were several brass-knobbed drawers where the cutlery was kept. The end draw was full of odds and ends, tops, pistols, string, odd gloves, etc. On the wide bench underneath, stood all the family's boots and shoes, of all shapes and sizes.

There were two scrubbed wooden tables, and it was a delight to poke out the dried soap from the cracks with a skewer. This was done when grown-ups were not about. Some pegs for hats and jackets were in one corner, under which stood my beloved rocking horse. In the opposite corner was a large cupboard, in the top half of which was kept the everyday china, mainly made of a crinkly china, with a small pink rose, and also odd plates. Underneath, in a separate cupboard, was our toy cupboard. There lived my Noah's Ark and all its in habitants. Even today Ayrshire cows are referred to, by me, as 'Noah's Ark' cows. A farmyard was my pride and joy, with all its little metal hurdles and farm animals. There were several board games and a little wheeled horse, with a painted saddle and a bridle of blue. The floor of the room was of faded orange and yellow square bricks or tiles, very much worn, and covered by coconut matting. Before the range lay a rag rug made from odd bits of material, usually of dark hue.

Every Friday the kitchen floor was scrubbed with Sunlight soap. The mats were taken up, shaken and, if it was fine, dragged along the grass to freshen them. I would sit on a mat while Tom Parker, the cowman, pulled the mat the length of the 'green'. I am afraid, today, it would take a couple of Tom Parkers to pull the mats and me!

The kitchen was a favourite room, as a kitchen should be. The range kept a warm glow, and there would be delicious bakings of cakes and pies, also the smell of freshly-washed linen being ironed with flat irons heated on the range. Mrs Rolph, the horsekeeper's wife, was an artiste with those flat irons. She was tall and slim, with a lovely complexion and hair caught up in a bun. She wore a coarse sacking apron at times, and no queen wore her gown with more grace. She came from Suffolk, and we would sit, fascinated, as she spat on the iron to test its heat, and told us stories of her childhood whilst, under her skilled hands, sheets, pillowcases, shirts, undergarments, handkerchiefs and all manner of household linen, were made into neat smooth piles ready for linen cupboard and drawers.

In very cold weather we were bathed ina tin bath in front of the kitchen fire, big fluffy towels warming on the fender. Should we be unwell, quite often we would be tucked up in a big old armchair and put by the fire. There would be dogs and kittens vying for the warmest positions, until Mother needed more space and would put them out, saying, 'That dog will go blind staring at the fire'. I don't think they ever did, and as soon as her back was turned they would be back sitting by the fire.

On winter evenings we would play in the kitchen, and friends would come in to join us. Here is an extract from a letter from Cis Izzard (née Peat), who was a friend of my brother, Alfred, and sister, Margaret. She lived in one of the cottages with her mother, father, sisters and brothers. I still receive letters from her and her sister, Nellie, and brother, Stanley, and they bring back a picture of Priestley as I remember it.

'I have lovely memories of playing with Margaret and Alfred in that lovely warm kitchen. Your mother gave us bread and dripping for our supper and cocoa to drink. There were great joints of meat in those days, from which came a great deal of dripping.'

She also mentions a magic lantern show given by Alfred in the back room with a lantern in which a candle had to be put to light it. I can so well picture the scene, in that old kitchen, with lamplight shining down on the children grouped round the fire with their mugs of cocoa and their bread and dripping, girls in pinafores and button boots, with glossy beribboned hair, and the boys in short trousers, all chattering about the lantern show they had just seen, and things they planned to do the next day. Outside, in the darkness, the wind moaned in the old weeping elm, and owls hooted in the nearby wood. When there was silence in the kitchen, one could hear the crickets which lived in a hole in the brickwork at the back of the kitchen range.

There would be stories told of ghosts on those dark winter evenings in the kitchen, so that when the time came to leave the lamplight and set out for their homes, the girls would become scared, the boys would become suddenly brave and stride manfully out, but ready to run at the sound of any unusual movements in the bushes.

One door from the kitchen led into a long hall with a door to the right leading to the dairy. Above this door was the row of bells which, years ago, summoned the servants from the kitchen to the dining room or bedroom, or wherever they were needed. Some of the bells still worked, and we pulled the cords in various rooms just to startle anyone standing near them. But quite often they stuck and their jangling ringing would break the silence at most odd times, and we were the startled ones.

The dairy was below ground level and stone steps led down to two rooms, the first of which was used as a cool room where bread, cheese, pickles, etc. were stored. Here jellies were put to set and cold meats reposed under their flyproof mesh covers. There were also bowls of pork and beef dripping. On special occasions there would be trifles, stiff with sherry and homemade raspberry jam, and topped with thick, whipped cream, pink succulent ham in its coat of golden breadcrumbs, a jellied tongue, a ripe Stilton with a pristine white starched napkin about its middle, and, in a crock nearby, crusty white loaves.

In the summer, Mother kept the homemade lemonade on a shelf in that dairy. It was served from a long-necked glass bottle with a tall glass stopper. The lemonade glugged cool and sharp when poured into a glass. I know now that the lemonade jug was a claret jug, which is still in my possession, and is now used for claret on special occasions, but, somehow, the 'glug' does not sound quite the same.

Through an opening on the same floor-level was the dairy proper. The floor was of brick, with a drain in the centre. Steps led up to a door, and gratings let in the air and light, keeping the dairy cool and sweet, cool in summer, very cold in winter. Hooks from a beam in the ceiling held rabbits and chickens waiting to be prepared for the table, goose or turkey for Christmas. In the shooting season, there would be pheasant, partridge and hares, if Father and Richard had been out with a shooting party.

Round the walls was wide shelving, some of lead, where the hams were put to cure before going away to be smoked. Others were of wooden slats, on which stood large, white, enamel pans for milk. The milk was poured into the pans from the large shining pails each milking and allowed to stand overnight. Each morning the milk was skimmed to take off the cream, which had risen to the top. The was done with a saucer-shaped dish full of holes, with a handle on one side, usually made of enamel, although older ones were of brass. This was called a skimmer, and was skilfully drawn across the top of the pan of milk just below the crust of cream. The milk would seep through the holes leaving the thick cream behind.

In spring, when the grass was lush, the cream would be very thick and the yellow bowl was soon full. In winter, with poorer grass and cows on dry feed, the cream would be much thinner. Each day the jug was filled with cream for use in the kitchen and at the table.

On another shelf stood the jugs of milk for use in the house. When we were babies, Mother had a special jug for each of us. I can remember just the two: one was a fat, orange jug, with a band of white on which there were flowers. That one, I think, was mine. Richard's was a blue willow pattern. Usually one cow was chosen from the herd as a house cow, one that gave rich milk, high in butter-fat.

At one end of the dairy stood the old wooden butter-making barrels, slung between wooden stands and turned by a handle. The cream was poured in through a hole, which was then sealed with a bung. In those days the butter made was sold at market. However, during my time at Priestley, these were no longer in use. A square-shaped glass jar, with a wooden paddle suspended from a lid into the jar, was used for the little butter we used at home. The paddle was turned by an outside handle. During the war years this paddle broke and could not be replaced, so a little butter was made using a wire whisk, and finished off by hand, well scrubbed, I might add. To make the butter, the cream was put into the jar, or barrel, and churned with aching arms, cursed and pleaded with to 'come'. Then the magic sound as the texture of the cream changed to a sloshing sound, as the curds of butter came. The buttermilk was strained off. Cold spring water was pumped by hand into the sink and here the butter curds were washed many times. A little salt was added to the last washing, then a final squeezing of the butter to remove all the water. The soft butter oozed between the fingers as one squeezed hard to make sure all the water was out. Then followed the delightful task of making the butter into pounds, or half pounds, with wooden butter pats, deftly shaping each block, and adding a pattern as one fancied to each finished pat of butter.

Here is an extract from a letter I received:

'When we were small we came for the milk at the kitchen door, sometimes we bought a pound of that gorgeous dairy butter, of which I have never tasted such, since those days...'

Another woman who came to the door for milk, usually skimmed milk, was a Mrs Peddar who lived in the Warren Farm cottage about one and a half miles away. She was tall and wore rusty black. She never smiled, but handed me her can, which always seemed to house a black beetle or two. The beetles were tipped out, the can filled, and the penny taken. With a curt nod of her head, Mrs Peddar turned and began her long walk back to her lonely cottage.

Another dish to be found in the dairy was a large enamel piedish, into which would be poured the first milk from a freshly-calved cow. This was called beestings, and was cooked in the oven like a rice pudding.

The pantry was a square room, on the left of the kitchen. Wide wooden shelves lined the walls, under which were cupboards containing the best china, so very rarely used. Homemade jams and pickles were ranged along the upper shelves, raspberry, strawberry, plum, and black currant; jams glowing like jewels, and marmalade shining like captured sunlight.

Under the shelves were drawers, and in these were kept an assortment of treasures, napkins, doilies, old school books, dusters, brown paper and string. Along a wide shelf underneath were hockey sticks, skates, hockey boots, riding boots, tennis shoes and old racquets. Along one end of the pantry were large square biscuit tins full of flour, sugar, dried fruit and rice.

The floor was green lino, and in one corner was a round hole, known as the 'rat hole', but was really the hole through which, previously, had run a pipe down to the beer cellar below. It was my brothers' delight, when a new girl came to Priestley to help Mother in the house, to wait until she went into the pantry, and they would be in the beer cellar below, and poke a broom handle through the hole, thus frightening the poor girls almost to death.

What I remember most about the pantry was the large cracked cup standing on the shelf, which, in the spring, was filled with a revolting mixture of brimstone and treacle, a spoonful of which was ladled down our protesting throats each morning. This mixture was supposed to clear our blood and keep our skins spotless. I seem to remember my brother having his share of boils, and, during my 'teens, I bemoaned the usual outcrop of spots. Other medicines on the pantry shelf, and ladled out by Mother at any sign of flagging spirits, colds or tummy upsets, were syrup of figs, castor oil, senna pods, camphorated oil, Epsom salts, and the like. All of which, I might add, were given as very liberal doses and with a firm hand holding that large spoon. Vaseline, borasic powder and, of course, iodine for cuts and bruises and chilblains were all kept on hand.

A long passage led from the kitchen to a square hall, to the stairs to the left, and a door to the right, into the drawing room. Opposite this was a door leading down wooden steps to the beer cellar. Another door led out into the garden, and this was really the front of the house, but no one visiting used that door. The door, known as the front door, was along the passage opposite the garden door, and next to that was the dining room. The lino on the hall floor was black and white small squares, and seemed to stretch for miles along that hallway, especially when one was on one's knees scrubbing it. The square hall had a red and blue carpet on which stood the old oak coffer, which had been used as a cot for my great grandfather.

During the summer, Mother would fill an old, brown, glazed pottery jug which, at one time, had been used to carry beer to the men in the harvest fields, with deep crimson peonies. The door to the garden would be open, and all the scents of the garden would mingle with the Stephenson's furniture polish that was always used on the old furniture.

The beer cellar was very old and musty, brick-built with a brick floor. It consisted of one large room and two smaller rooms with shelves, which, no doubt, at one time, held the bottles of wine and barrels of beer. Apples were also stored there and it was a great 'dare' to go down to the cellar on dark winter nights, with a candle, to bring back an apple. During the spring there would be incubators filled with eggs for hatching, and a constant smell of warm oil from the lamps. The eggs had to be turned and sprinkled with water, and as the eggs hatched the cellar would be full of cheeping sounds from little, yellow, fluffy bodies. There were doors leading to a slope which led up to a grating into the garden. Originally, barrels of home-made beer would have been rolled into, and out of, the cellar in this way.

During the war, the beer cellar was strengthened with strong timber posts for use as an air-raid shelter. The first time the air-raid siren sounded, someone from Flitwick rang to let us know. I collected the dogs and cats, Mother scolded, and Father ushered us down those wooden steps into the fortified beer cellar. The 'phone rang again to say the All Clear had gone, and out we thankfully trooped. We never used the beer cellar as a shelter again, preferring to remain above ground when there was any danger of air raids. We were lucky living in the deep countryside, so different from the people in the cities who, night after night, spent their time in air-raid shelters.

The drawing-room was Mother's room, a square room with one window overlooking the cow meadow, and French windows leading into the garden. There was, at one time, a piano (my sister played) and the piano stool containing Church of England and Sankey & Moody hymn books, together with a large, deep settee and two armchairs. The carpet was black and grey, the settee and chairs deep green, with plum coloured cushions. A lovely mahogany table stood in the corner, on which were family photographs, and on the walls were paintings by my sister Margaret, the shades of blues and mauves showing the influence of Sylvester Stannard, under whom she studied art. There were hyacinths in pots on the window-sills in spring and a potted plant in summer and autumn. On the mantlepiece above the fireplace stood two black lustre vases.

Mother sat in the drawing room on Sunday afternoons with her library book and a box of Black Magic chocolates. Father sat in the dining room, and slept. But about four o'clock one would hear him flapping (he wore old rubber-soled bowling shoes and socks held up by suspenders, one of which had usually come adrift and flapped along the floor), along the hall to the drawing room for a dip into the box of chocolates. These chocolates were the only thing to tempt us into the drawing room, just one chocolate each. We had to sit quietly, and it seemed, if we moved a muscle, it was 'mind my black vases'. We could not sit still a minute and were out of that room as soon as we possibly could. Mother could never understand why I did not want to sit quietly there with her, but, as cats and dogs were barred, it was no place for me. I still have those black vases to remind me. They are of a shiny black glaze, made in about 1830, when many black articles were the fashion for the mourning of Prince Albert.

The piano was sold after Margaret was married as there was no one to play it, and with it went the Sankey hymnals. I can still remember Margaret playing the piano, and my brothers gleefully singing:
'There is a Happy Land Far Far Away
            Where little piggies play
all live long day
'til they see the butcher come
            to cut three slices off their bum
Far Far Away ...'

The sound of Mother advancing caused us to run far far away, very quickly!

The dining room was on the right on entering through the front door. This room was the one most used, apart from the kitchen. Here we did our homework at the big, polished, oak table, here meals were eaten when guests were staying, and always Christmas supper was served here. An oil lamp hung from the ceiling, a lamp which , each morning, had to be refilled with paraffin oil, have the wick trimmed and the glass chimney cleaned. Even with all this care, the lamp sometimes flared and smoked, leaving a sooty ring on the ceiling. This usually meant a new mantle was needed. In one corner of the room was our pride and joy – a gramaphone – a large wind-up machine with a lid at the top and a cupboard underneath, where the records were kept, each record embellished with the white terrier dog listening at a gramaphone horn, and labelled 'His Master's Voice'. We had such records as 'Felix Kept on Walking', 'Over the Garden Wall', and so on. The majority of the records were bought for sixpence each. Often the handle of the gramaphone had to be swiftly turned as the singer's voice and music whined slower and slower. The gramaphone needles were kept in a little tin, and had to be changed regularly, taking care not to drop any in case we ran one into our foot. On the table, by the window, stood another delight – a radio. This was run on glass accumulators, which had to be recharged each week. Most Saturdays would see those who owned a wireless, walking, or cycling, back from the village garage with the recharged accumulator, leaving another one to be put on charge during the coming week to be ready for the following Saturday. Often, a little square wooden box would be strapped to the carrier over the bicycle's rear wheel. The precious accumulator would stand in this and be carried safely home. Many early firelit evenings were spent listening to Uncle Mac, the Mayor and Larry the Lamb, also to Henry Hall's Danceband – 'And this is Henry Hall speaking'. Billy Cotton and his band were a great favourite, especially as the Cottons once lived at Daphne Villa, Kings Road, Flitwick. Except for very special occasions the wireless was never switched on until evening, even when we had an electric radio, apart from listening to the News. Father seemed to think it a mortal sin to have the radio on when we were working. I hate to think what he would have said today, when people seem to be unable to work unless the radio is on, full blast.

Along the wall of the dining room stood the sideboard, on which stood a few silver-plated pieces, and a candelabra which, as a small boy, my brother Richard delighted in cleaning. In the two cupboards were glasses, bottles of drinks and Mother's workbasket. I would curl up on the rug by the glowing fire, the lamplight gleaming on the polished oak and the silver, and listen whilst Mother read to me. 'Black Beauty' was my favourite, and Father dozing in his armchair would explain certain words to me. Charles Dickens' 'Old Curiosity Shop' was another book Mother read to me. Both these books are so sad, and yet throughout the years they have remained great favourites of mine.

Some evenings there would be friends of my parent to play bridge, and I would either play in the kitchen with Elsie, who lived in one of the cottages, or be tucked up early in bed with a special treat of scrambled eggs on toast, and allowed to read for a while.

In the kitchen a tray of dainty sandwiches was made ready for the guests, and a pot of proper ground coffee, specially purchased from The Cadena, Bedford. The coffee was served in small, thin, china cups. At other times, the only coffee used was Camp coffee, a bottle of which, for some reason, always stood on the shelf above the kitchen range.

In the dining room, near the fireplace, were two deep leather chairs, Richard's little brass-studded stool, and my chair. Father's desk was in one corner, with a glass-fronted bookcase above it. In Father's desk cupboard, were boxes of cigars and cartridges for his gun. We were never allowed to touch these cupboards, but the odour of cigars and the cedar-wood box in which were kept the dominoes, wafted out when Father opened the door, and mingled with the scents of polish, wood fire burning, and the bowl of flowers or bulbs.

At the window, as well as lace curtains, there were green blinds to be pulled down on hot summer days, so keeping the room cool and dim. But in winter, when the wind howled and sleet lashed at the windows, the wooden shutters would be pulled up and then then all was safe and cosy. No wonder we all loved the old dining room. Such happy times the family spent there all together.

The stairs led from the hall to the square landing above, over which presided a painting of Alfred Medlock, a forbidding ancestor. At the top of the stairs was a window with square glass panes and whenever we looked back at this window from across the fields, we imagined we could see a 'face' watching us. Off the landing were the four bedrooms. The first bedroom , the spare room, with a window overlooking the cow meadow, was the best bedroom, with a large double bed (feather mattress, of course), wash stand with cut glass jugs and basin, and, I swear, though no one believes me, a glass chamber pot. But perhaps I did imagine it! Along one wall was a huge tallboy with a looking-glass in the door, so, turning over in bed, it frightened the life out of you to see a face staring back at you. Candlelight played funny tricks there as well. A carved mahogany dressing-table stood in one corner, and in another was a cupboard for hanging clothes. Mother kept her best clothes here. One of our many cats also made her way to this cupboard, and, in one of Mother's resplendent hats, in its cocoon of tissue paper, found the perfect bed for the birth of her kittens. Several days passed before Mother calmed down!

I was not very fond of that room. But, as it had a double bed, when friends of mine stayed the night we slept there. Such plans we made, and secrets shared, tucked beneath snug blankets and cuddled deep in the feather bed. One friend often stayed the night, and together we named the bed 'the bugs' abode'.

Next door was Mother and Father's room. This had two windows, one overlooking the yards, and from this window, early in the morning, Father would give his order to the foreman waiting below. There was a fireplace in this room in which, during very severe weather, or illness, a fire would be lit. I still remember lying cosily between lavender-scented sheets watching the flickering firelight. Mother's dressing table was in one corner, the drawers of which, when opened, smelled of lavender-water and Ponds face cream. The large chest of drawers, with a cupboard above, housed undergarments, best linen, and all spiced with lavender. In one compartment Mother kept a doll, once the treasured possession of my late sister, Margaret. The china doll had flaxen hair and blue eyes, and on one hand each finger had been snapped off. Whenever Margaret upset Alfred, he would snatch up her doll and break off a finger. As can be imagined, bedlam then broke out, and so the doll was removed for safety.

The small room adjoining was used as a nursery. The window overlooked the yards and stables. Around the wall was a frieze of little Dutch boys and girls sitting on a fence with windmills in the distance. The little white-painted iron bedstead stood against one wall, and was made up with its feather mattress and feather pillows and bolster, snow-white sheets (flannelette in winter) and thick yellow woollen blankets, topped with a pretty patterned eiderdown. A hot-water bottle of rubber or stone would have warmed the bed before one climbed in. The blue and white curtains to match the blue trousers and white blouses of the Dutch children would be closed. There, snug and warm, listening to the stamp of horses' hooves on the cobbled stable floor, sleep came sweetly. Opposite the bed stood a chest of drawers on which was placed a candle, and that ghastly concoction Mother swore by, a large bottle of syrup of figs and a very large serving spoon.

On the other side of the landing was the room overlooking the garden. This was the boys' room until they married. It then became my bedroom. A long narrow passage ran to the back of the house, on the left of which was a small square room. This was my sister's bedroom, opposite which was the chimney-breast of the boys' bedroom. My brothers hid behind this chimney-breast, jumping out on any unsuspecting person coming along the dark, lino-covered passage. I have never heard of anyone dying there of shock, but there were some very nervous folk around.

The large bathroom had a barred window. I presume it had once been the nursery, as a window in the passage almost opposite was also barred. There was a fireplace in the bathroom, and in winter, if we had visitors staying, there would be a glowing coal fire burning. Mostly, when young, we were bathed in a tin bath before the kitchen range. But as we grew older, we bathed and froze in the bathroom 'proper', hurrying to wrap ourselves in the large soft bath towels, warm from the linen cupboard.

At the end of the passage were two rooms, a small box-room and a larger room overlooking the garden. This room was supposed to be our nursery-cum-playroom and housed a large, brass double bed, complete with brass knobs and a huge, fat, feather mattress. There were large chests containing christening robes, and other long-forgotten finery. In other dark cupboards there were scrapbooks and postcard albums. My doll's house was there, and a large china doll ina pink satin frock and a large pink bow in her silly, blond curly hair. (I had straight, mousy-coloured hair, and was not doll-minded at all!) I did not like that room one bit. It always seemed to have a brooding and listening air about it. The box-room next to it was small, with one window overlooking the roof to the office below. It was, as its name implies, full of boxes or to be more exact, cases and trunks. My brother's tuckbox was kept there during the school holidays, and great gloom descended when it was brought downstairs and packed with his going-back-to-school goodies. But there was great excitement when the trunks were dragged out and dusted for our holidays by the sea. The little tugboat with two funnels, which once belonged to my older brother, and my red-keeled yacht, with her white sails, were cleaned up and new string added where required, and packed together with our bathing costumes.

Priestley Farm house was a wonderful home for us children to be brought up in, with plenty of space to run wild. There was a lovely garden, set out with lawns and flowerbeds, apple trees and, before I was born, a cheery tree. I was always most upset that I missed that! There were raspberries and strawberries, asparagus beds and, right at the bottom of the garden, a small hazel coppice. A magnificent weeping elm grew just inside the garden gate where, in summer, we slung a hammock in which we spent many lazy hours until tipped out. Alas, the weeping elm eventually succumbed to Dutch Elm disease.

Roses and honeysuckle rambled over the house walls, whilst the west side of the house was clad with ivy, the nesting place of many sparrows.

*My Mother standing by the old weeping elm at Priestley, 1947.*
*Unfortunately this lovely tree succumbed to Dutch Elm Disease.*

Mother loved her garden, and during hot dry summer evenings would water her beloved plants with water she had saved from the washing, etc., getting us to help carry the rather smelly water to the farthest parts of the garden.

My sister, Margaret, was very fond of tennis, so Father had a tennis court laid out for her. Many were the tennis parties enjoyed on that slightly bumpy court, those watching, sitting on a daisy-strewn bank at one end. Beyond the tennis court was the orchard, with very old fruit trees. I especially remember an ancient crooked, damson trees, with moss-covered trunk, wonderful for us to climb. It was in the hedge bordering the orchard that the yellow gage trees grew. There was also, in the corner, a tall pear tree which bore the sweetest of little pears. The five-barred gate leading into the orchard was the favourite spot for us to balance, between its bars, our plank for a see-saw.

A bank sloped down from the hedge, and it was here Mother had her washing line, the washed linen blowing in the wind vying with the daisies scattering the grass below for whiteness. When we were very small, we loved to roll down this bank, our noses filled with the fresh soapy smell of the washing mixed with the crushed grass and flowers. How steep that little bank seemed to us.

# Chapter Four

# Happy Days

## Off to the Sea

How true is the quotation ...

'To travel hopefully is a better thing than to arrive'

*(R L Stevenson)*

There was great excitement when it was decided to venture forth for our holiday by the sea, nearly always Yarmouth, Lowestoft or Gorleston, for a fortnight. Mother must have girded up her loins beforehand and, should there have been such things as tranquilizers in those days, she would have resorted to bottlesful. We were not easy children to cope with away from home. I can remember being told that Mother stayed a month at Gorleston with Richard, when he was a small boy recovering from a bad bout of whooping cough. Every and all day, he insisted on standing to watch the road being repaired. He had designs on the steamroller; his whooping cough was cured, but Mother's legs were never the same again.

We were in a great state of excitement leading up to the day of departure. Then, as the great day loomed near, I decided I did not want to go. How could the harvest be got in without me? How would the horses, dogs, cats, etc. exist if I wasn't there? Anyway, I hated travelling, I was always ill. However, in spite of my protests, I was bundled into the car, plus a large tin in case of problems from my queasy tummy, and off we sped at a very sedate speed, Father at the wheel. The conversation was very limited. It ran between, 'I feel sick', 'I am going to be sick', 'I have been sick', and, 'When shall we see the sea?' Father would point out the changing colour of the corn as we neared Norfolk or Suffolk where the ears of wheat became more red than the golden wheat of Priestley.

Once at our destination and installed, my time was spent watching or riding on the donkeys or ponies, watching every performance of Punch and Judy, or sailing my boat on the pond in the Winter Gardens. I was terrified of the sea and howled whenever it was suggested I got more than my feet wet. What is more, I came out in great heat bumps, and I itched. For the first day or two we remained wrapped up in layers of clothes.

Each day a garment was removed so that we should get acclimatized to the sea air. By the time the sea air got to me I was beyond caring. I was covered in spots, which were covered in calamine lotion, or rubbed with carbolic soap. But I still itched!

*The author in hat actually daring to sit in sea water. Looks as if the spots are causing trouble as usual. Her friend, Pat, is the happy one.*

One of the treats was a trip from Gorleston to the Sparrows' Nest at Lowestoft. On one occasion Mother must have been beyond thinking straight; she took us on the *bus*. Both Richard and I were promptly sick – we all walked back.

There were good times; lovely sand castles we built, and, at least for one evening, we were allowed to sit up late to walk along the promenade to see the strings of lights and to listen to the band playing on their illuminated bandstand. Out at sea, ships would have flashing lights and the sound of the dark waves slapping against the shore was all pure magic, and I have never forgotten the thrill of it.

*Happy to be mounted on this toy horse at one of our seaside holidays.*

During the mornings, we would play on the beach whilst the grownups reclined in deck chairs, for which they had purchased tickets from a man in charge of all the chairs on that part of the beach. During the morning a man would come along with a tray supported by straps around his neck. On this tray were such delights as windmills, wooden spades, little tin shapes to make all manner of sandpies, coloured balls and many other small purchases. As we made our way to the beach there would also be a 'Stop me and buy one' Walls Ice Cream cart. We were usually allowed one such treat, so it was great fun choosing a flavour. But my pocket money always went on the ponies. Some afternoons we were taken to a restaurant for a shrimp tea. That was not to my liking. I could not, and still cannot, bear the sight of those poor, popping, little black eyes!

Happy the day we packed to return home, spots and all. What a relief to turn down the stoney road to Priestley and find all was well, the dogs pleased to see us and, though some of the fields were now stubble, still quite a bit of corn standing in shocks to cart to the stack yard. There were kind hands to anoint the itching spots, which itched less away from the sea air. We soon recovered from our holidays. Mother and Father, no doubt exhausted by it all, took themselves off elsewhere for a few days' peace and quiet.

## High Days and Holidays

Apart from Christmas there were other 'High Days' to remember. The day my sister, Margaret, married William Billington was a great day at Priestley. A marquee had been erected on the lawn and caterers hired to provide the wedding breakfast. There had been such polishing and tidying of the house and farm for months before the wedding day. As well as to-ing and fro-ing to the dressmakers there were visits to town, shopping, which did not please me at all. Margaret was much loved and the church was filled with guests. Afterwards, Margaret and Bill, with the bridesmaids and her pet terrier, Judy, had their photographs taken in one of the farm carts, drawn by Daisy, a chestnut Suffolk punch mare. Daisy had been groomed to perfection and her brasses and harness shone to match the occasion. All the men of the farm were entertained in the evening at the Victory Hall, Flitwick, where a meal had been laid on for them. It was a great and happy day for all.

At Easter time we ate spicy hot-cross buns early on Good Friday morning, baked by Mr Howlet, the baker at Westoning, and collected by Mr Bass, who worked on the farm, walking from Westoning across the plank bridge to start work at seven o'clock in the morning. On Good Fridays all farm work stopped at twelve noon, apart from the afternoon milking, and there seemed to settle over Priestley a special kind of stillness, something one cannot quite describe. Perhaps some lingering presence of long ago? In the afternoon, primroses would be gathered from the woods; in some places the woods were open to the village people to allow them to gather bunches of primroses to decorate the church or dress the graves.[1] I have only to bury my nose in a bunch of creamy yellow primroses, with their cool pink stalks, for the memories to come flooding back of gathering the sweet-smelling bunches from beneath the trees in Flitwick Wood. Afterwards, in her cottage by the wood, (once a gamekeeper's cottage), Mrs Pressland gave us lemonade and a slice of her home-made fruit cake.

*My Sister, Margaret and her husband, William Billington, after their wedding in 1934. Daisy, the Suffolk Punch pulls the cart through the stack-yard with bridesmaids, best man, and Judy, the dog, all turned out to perfection. Front left, Margaret, Elsie Stock, me holding the dog, Irene Gazeley, who married my brother Alfred. Back right, Alfred Cole (my Brother), Kathie Billington. Front right, William Billington.*

1 There is a delightful description of 'dressing the graves' on Easter eve, in the classic 'Kilvert's Diary' by Francis Kilvert.

Easter Sunday was much looked forward to. Apart from the lovely Easter hymns and the church so bright with flowers, when we came down to breakfast in the kitchen, on the dresser, among the blue and white crockery, stood our chocolate Easter Eggs, all wrapped in gaily-patterned silver paper, with yellow ribbon and fluffy chickens. For dinner there would be roast lamb and mint sauce, and Mother's special trifle. In the orchard, quite often, there would be a coop with a proud mother hen with her brood of cheeping, newly-hatched chicks. Somehow it seems the sun always shone at Easter, but however early I rose, I did not see the 'sun dance', as one is supposed to early on Easter Sunday morn. We searched the banks for the first of the violets and poked about in hedges for the sight of a nest being built.

An outing very much enjoyed about Easter time was a visit to the Hertfordshire Hunt's Point-to-Point meeting at Friars Wash. Here every other person one met was a friend. The horses entered for the races were good honest hunters, some even doing a job of work on the farm at times. The race course was over natural country of grass and ploughed fields with cut and laid hedges. The picnic basket taken to these Point-to-Points was filled to bursting with home-baked bread and pastries. There would be plenty of drinks of all kinds, and at each car there would be an invitation to join in and have a drink whilst the merits of so-and-so's mount would be discussed. In earlier days there would have been the Farmers' Tent, where the Hunt Master entertained the farmers over whose land he had hunted during the season. From stories I have been told, this was indeed the highlight of the day. A large quantity of food and drink was enjoyed by all invited.

Sometimes, during the summer months, a cricket match would be arranged between a Priestley Eleven, captained by my brother, Richard, and an Eversholt team. This match was much looked forward to by all the men. Harry, who did many of the odd jobs about the farm, was scrubbed up by his workmates and given a new outfit of second-hand clothes to grace such an occasion. I don't think it mattered too much about the final score; there was a lovely summer evening, the crack of the ball meeting bat, and good-tempered barracking as the ball was despatched to the boundary, chased by an outfielder who, at that moment, had been engaged in conversation with an onlooker on the merits of his potato crop. There would be a great cheer when a catch was taken, or the opposition clean-bowled. As the shadows lengthened over the pitch, play drew to a close, and both teams made their way to the bar of the Green Man Public House opposite the field, to celebrate, win or lose. The game had been played with enjoyment by all the players and bystanders alike.

## School Days

I first went to school at a little private school in Flitwick, Miss Constance Hetley's Flitwick High School. The school was in a long building, which lay back from the High Street. A narrow lilac-tree-lined path led up to the school, which had a paddock to the rear where we played and had drill (now called Physical Education) each morning. We marched proudly up and down on Empire Day, and in the summer made hay-houses of the cut grass among the gorsebushes. In the school-room were tables and chairs, desks, cupboards, pegs for coats, a blackboard and a 'tortoise' stove, which kept us all warm. Miss Hetley warmed her dinner, which always smelt delicious, in a tin basin on this stove.

In this school-room we were soundly taught all subjects, including German, French and some Latin. Here I acquired the love of poetry. We were also taught how to sew, paint and sing. Although I found such lesson difficult, I loved the afternoons when, busy with the dreaded sewing, we began stitching a cat marked out on cardboard with dots; if I remember rightly, I insisted it should be sewn with mauve thread. We then proceeded to table mats, sewn in all colours, and moccasins in green and cream raffia. As we worked, Miss Hetley read to us. What stories she read. Spellbound, we listened in that cosy room, with the darkening world outside.

On the windowsill were boxes with wet flannel for cress seeds, or paste pots, in which peas and beans were set, so that we could watch them grow. We were taken on nature walks, with picnics in summer. A treat we all looked forward to was a picnic and cricket match on the Ramblers Cricket Ground, which was situated beyond Froghall Farm, Flitwick. A truly great adventure. Once we were taken to Bedford, to the theatre, to watch Shakespeare's 'A Midsummer Night's Dream'.

For some of the time that I attended Miss Hetley's school, I rode my pony, Beauty, to school each day, starting from Priestley in good time, with my satchel on my back, containing my lunch. Beauty was stabled at the Swan Inn by the station, and I would go to her at lunch time to give her a feed of hay and make sure she had water. After school, we would trot home to Priestley.

What a wonderful woman Miss Hetley was! She gave a sound grounding of education to so many children, and I, for one, am eternally grateful for all the patience she showed to me.

Eventually, I went to Bedford High School, travelling each day from Flitwick Station, to which I cycled from Priestley, complete with gas mask (it was during the Second World War), satchel, hockey stick and boots, or a tennis racquet, depending on the season. I would wait, with other school-children, for the eight o'clock train each morning, and it was with a sigh of relief that Mr Shrives, the Station Master, saw the train depart with its noisy, effervescent load of children and, of course, the more sedate passengers.

I never found lessons easy, and would dash home, throwing down my school hat and satchel, and rush out on to the farm, with Mother's voice floating from far off, that dreaded word 'Homework'! I know now I should have taken heed.

Years later, after my Father died and we had left Priestley, I went back to Miss Hetley's school as an assistant. I loved those few years helping with the young children. One of the many happy memories I have whilst helping there, is of one February morning, when Jennifer, Jacqueline and Richard Westrope, the three small children of Mr and Mrs Westrope, who then lived at Priestley, arrived at the school, their rosy faces beaming. I recall that the girls had their hair in plaits, and Richard wore a school cap at a jaunty angle. They all came running up to me, and in their fists they clutched bunches of snowdrops picked for me from Priestley. I buried my face in their bunches of flowers so that they could not see my tears. I remembered so well the hazel trees beneath which the snowdrops grew and how, at their age, I had picked bunches of snowdrops from under these trees to take to school.

## Reminiscing and Childhood

### i)  Fruit, Flowers and Shows

Each season of the year hold memories for us all. Apart from the work carried out on the farm, other memories flood back to me. Scents and sounds send time spinning back, and when I bend down to smell the old-fashioned roses blooming in my Wiltshire garden I am once again back at Priestley, sitting on the old wooden steps leading to the French windows of the drawing-room. A light breeze wafts the scent of pink cabbage roses, mingled with cut hay. And from the kitchen comes the mouth-watering smell of dinner cooking and Mother's voice calling along the passage for me to come and set the table for dinner.

Gooseberries, plump and hairy, remind me of the gooseberry bushes that grew along by the stable wall and garden fence, where the nettles grew thickly, but at the time of gathering, Tom Parker, with his scythe, mowed down the nettles, thus saving us from stung legs. I hated picking the gooseberries, which were a very spiteful variety with sharp thorns. Armed with enamel colanders and china basins, we sallied forth under protest. But I did not mind topping and tailing the fruit once it was picked, and I was there at the ready when Mother served up a boiled suet gooseberry pudding, hot from its cloth-covered basin, and then coated with brown sugar and cream. Shelling peas was another occupation I quite enjoyed, sitting under the old weeping elm tree, dreaming away as I slit open fat-podded peas, some with wiggling maggots, which were hastily removed.

Of the flowers, sweetpeas, I think, have the most evocative scent, and once again I am transported back in time to the flower tent at the local agricultural show, walking among vases of perfect blooms of sweetpeas, sprays of roses, or single blooms of pure perfection, and little pots of pansy faces, and the stately gladioli. The vegetables on display were scrubbed clean; potatoes, round and kidney-shaped, perfectly matched on their parsley-lined plates. Ruddy beetroot were also there, and long, straight kidney beans that had spent the previous night wrapped in damp flannel to keep them fresh for the show. There were huge onions glistening with just a hint of vaseline, big-hearted crisp green cabbage, and creamy, curded cauliflowers. The striped marrows, not too big but just the right size for the dinner table, were displayed with pride. They always reminded me of fat contented piglets. Then, on to the preserves section, the jams and pickles, all neatly hatted with coloured covers and labelled, the jams glowing with the summer sunshine contained within their fruits – raspberry and strawberry jams, all bright, and the blackcurrant jam, dark and mysterious. The early fruit piled on their paper doilies – redcurrants, raspberries, strawberries and golden gooseberries. Why, I wonder, couldn't my Father grow gooseberries like these instead of our green bullet-like ones? Apparently, we were not into dessert gooseberries.

I move on in memory to the clever flower arrangements to represent some chosen theme, and the classes for wild flowers (there were plenty to gather in those days before the advent of wholesale weed killers), which were entered by school children. All this infusion of scents mixed with the smell of the trampled grass beneath the canvas marquee. I recall the sound of hushed voices of those discussing various exhibits as to why they thought so-and-so should have got first prize and not second for his or her exhibit.

I recall the brown, weather-beaten faces above spotlessly clean collars, boots specially polished for the day out, and the women in pretty print frocks and straw hats, looking anxiously at the cake section to see how so-and-so's sponge had 'cut'. Mostly sponge cakes stand firm and light and even, but maybe just an odd one had sunk a tiny bit in the middle. 'Well', they would say, 'I wouldn't have put that on show'.

The Bedfordshire Agricultural Show was one of the great occasions and Ampthill Park was at one time the show ground, but, in later years it was moved to Bedford. For weeks before the day of the show, cattle, horses, pigs, sheep and poultry would be 'got ready for the show'. Extra grooming, feeding and handling took place. The mares and foals were trotted up and down so that they knew how they should behave. The harness was polished and carts and wagons given an extra coat of paint. Pigs were scrubbed and cosseted. My husband's grandfather, who farmed at Thrupp End, Lidlington, had a black-and-white sow who gave birth to eight black, and eight white piglets a few days before the show day. Someone sat with the sow day and night to make sure she did not overlay them (lie on them). I believe, after all that trouble, she did actually win first prize in her class. Her prowess was, and still is, much discussed to this day by the family.

On the great day itself, it seemed that every farmer, farmworker and family gathered at the show. Seedsmen had their tents with chairs and tables, where weary-footed wives of farmers and growers, who were customers, could refresh themselves with tea, whilst their husbands took something a little stronger.

There were trade stands with new elevators brightly painted, ladders, mowing machines and such implements as the farm world required, but not too many stands. Mostly people wanted to see the grand parade of the winning animals. A great cheer went up for the local winners. The big Shires responded to the shouts and clapping by trotting out with their great hooves, as if they were thistledown, whilst the stately cow, with her championship rosette or her horns, suddenly decided she was a heifer again and set off at a gallop with her herdsman being towed along at the end of her halter. The draught horses, with traces clinking, trotted solemnly by, while the Hackneys picked up their knees to their noses and sped daintily round the ring. Everyone seemed to know everyone else, and each had his favourites to cheer on.

The beer tent was very popular, and as the day drew to a close, bursts of song issued forth. Old marching songs, popular songs and 'To be a Farmer's Boy' could be heard.

On the way home, we passed horses and foals being led back to their stables, some proudly bearing winners' rosettes. Pigs, sheep and lambs were loaded into various carts pulled by a farm cob, securely covered by a net, and driven home. Some were loaded into cattle-wagons and driven home in style, all, no doubt, glad to be back in their own sty or pasture. By us humans, the day was talked over for many weeks to come.

Today, the agricultural shows are very large. There is an enormous amount of trade stands, and so much mechanisation. But the grand parade still draws the crowd. The agricultural worker, be he stockman, horsekeeper or shepherd, still shows with pride, the best of his profession.

## ii) Early Memories of Flitwick Mill

Flitwick is still lucky enough to have a mill, probably standing on the same site as the one mentioned in the Domesday Book, standing on the banks of the River Flit, whose waters once turned the overshot iron water-wheel to grind the corn between the millstones housed in the mill. The present mill is owned by Mr John Goodman, in whose family the mill has been for many generations.

I have very early recollections of being taken to the mill in a pony and float, no doubt to collect some meal, and being carried up a flight of steps to see the millstones grinding. I have a vague memory of dust, noise, the smell of crushed corn, and of wooden boards polished smooth by much sweeping. I was probably struck dumb by the thought that I might be ground up into pieces even smaller than I was already; I had a vivid imagination as a child, which ran riot at such times.

Another mill I can remember was at Greenfield. This mill was also worked by the waters of the Flit. A Mr Goodard was the miller here, and I used to see him with his daughter working there as I rode across the ford nearby. A few years ago, I walked along Mill Lane, Greenfield, thinking to see the old mill, and was surprised and disappointed to find a housing estate and a modern brickbuilt house where once, long ago, I watched the miller and his daughter working.

## iii) The Harvest Moon

In September, when the harvest had been taken, the fields of stubble lay waiting for the plough. The chicken house, with the young pullets about to lay, would be taken and set up on one of the stubble fields quite a way from the farm house. There, during the day, the young birds were free to roam and pick up the corn dropped among the stubble and any other delicacies their beaks might fancy. It was my job to see they were safely shut up each night.

One night I had been in bed for some time when I suddenly realised I had forgotten to shut up the chickens. Looking out of the bedroom window, I saw the full harvest moon lighting up the fields as if it were day-time. Quickly I pulled on a jumper over my pyjamas, slipped into wellington boots, grabbed a halter, and ran to the field where my pony, Ranger, grazed, and his constant companion, my mongrel dog, Zipp joined us. I whistled to Ranger, slipped the halter over his head, climbed onto his back and set off through a silent moonlight world to the chicken house. The beauty of that night still remains with me, the sharp tang of bruised mayweed growing among the stubble crushed by the pony's hooves, the silence of the empty fields, every twig and lead bathed in soft light from the big, round, golden moon, the pricked black-tipped ears of

*The author on Ranger, the pony who would come when called and on whom she rode over the moonlit fields to shut up the chickens. He was also a good gymkhana pony, winning many rosettes.*

that dear bay pony with whom I shared so much pleasure, the rusty-coloured, fox-like dog at his heels, and, from the spinney, came the hoot of an owl, with the sound of a train in the far distance. We cantered smoothly over to the chicken house where, apart from a sleepy squawk, all was well. With the chickens safely shut in, we returned to the farm house as swiftly and as silently as we had left.

### iv) *The Games We Played*

As the long winter drew to a close and the spring evenings lengthened, we would be out of doors as long as possible. The first starshine and Mother's final call reluctantly sent us in. Hopscotch squares would be left, the favourite skimmer stone put in a safe place until next time. If we had been playing marbles, they would be gathered up into a bag specially made for them. Such a medley of colours those marbles, as if a rainbow had got caught up in a spun glass ball. The big marbles were used to 'shoot' with, and were called dubbs. On a flat surface a ring of about seven inches was drawn with a piece of chalk. Five yards away a line would be drawn, and each player would place a small coloured marble in the ring. Each player bowled his or her dubb to try and knock out the other marbles. Those knocked out of the ring became the bowler's property. There was quite an art in shooting the dubbs. A skilful flick of the thumb and the smaller marbles were sent flying. There would be much swapping of marbles, mostly done in a most secretive manner, as if pieces of gold were being exchanged.

Tops and hoops had been abandoned as winter games, but skipping was always in fashion, either alone, with a short rope which had gaily painted handles, or several children skipping together, two holding the handles and turning the skipping rope whilst two or three skipped. Mostly it was girls who skipped, chanting, 'Salt, Mustard, Vinegar, Pepper'. Should a long rope be used for skipping, the rope would be turned faster and faster, those skipping running in and out until one tripped the rope and stopped it. Then, those turning the rope had a turn at the skipping.

Games of tag were a great favourite. Any chasing about was enjoyed. Someone said, 'Youth is wasted on the young'. How I could do with some of that energy now! To choose who was to be 'He', all players would stand in a line and one person would say, pointing to each, themselves included ...

> 'Pennoth of chips
>> to grease your lips
> And out goes *you*'

until just one person was left, and that person would be 'He' to chase and catch the others.

Another of the chants for skipping or choosing a 'He' was …
> 'My mother said I never should
> > play with the gypsies in the wood
> For if I did my mother would say
> > Naughty girl to *disobey*'

The same ritual was used as the previous chant. On the word *disobey* falling on you, you dropped out.

There were plenty of places for hide and seek, trees to climb, and sheltered nooks in hedges to play house, using old bits of crockery found in some long-forgotten rubbish dump, some with pretty flowers intact. I well remember a bright-blue, dented enamel teapot, a great embellishment to our hidden house in the roots of an old elm tree.

From the walnut tree in the paddock, hung a strong cart-rope swing with a thick folded sack as a seat. Here the bravest would swing right up among the high branches of that glorious tree.

> 'I remember, I remember where I was
> > used to swing,
> And thought the air must rush as fresh
> > to swallows on the wing';
> > > *(Thomas Hood)*

Those not so brave swayed lazily to and fro, pushing with one toe on the ground, sleepily dreaming, smelling the sharp aromatic smell of crushed walnut leaves. Woebetide anyone who, having finished with the swing, left it dangling from the branch. The top and seat had to be flung up into the low crook of a branch so that no animal would get its head caught and choke to death.

A wooden five-barred gate let into the orchard, and, balanced on the last-but-one bar, was a broad plank used as a see-saw. Up and down gently we soared, unless there was someone a bit rough on the other end, then you were jerked down with a bump. In retaliation you threw their end up with gusto, throwing them smartly into the air to land, if they were lucky, on the see-saw with a resounding thump. Mostly, though, it was a gentle see-sawing to the rhyme of …

> 'I saw Esau sitting on a see-saw
> > How many S's in that?'

White daisies and buttercups carpeted the grass beneath our feet, swallows flew overhead, and the long summer holidays seemed to go on for ever. We climbed the gnarled apple trees in spring to smell the blossom, and in the autumn to pick the fruit. We shook the tree which bore the little sweet pears, nearly always scabby, but scrumptious. The gooseberry bushes were plundered for the sharp crunchy berries, with dire results – tummy ache!

Along the side of the holly-hedge field grew a sweet chestnut tree. During the autumn we vied with squirrels for the nuts, and burst open the needle-sharp cases to gouge the little sweet chestnuts from their velvet lining. Sometimes we took them home to roast in the bars of the kitchen range. Usually they came out more burnt than roasted. The horse-chestnuts had been looked over for conkers, large brown shiny nuts. The largest and hardest was chosen and holed with a red-hot skewer. Through the hole we would thread a strong piece of string, well-knotted. A game of conkers would then take place. The conker on the string was held at arm's length whilst an opponent struck it with his largest conker trying to break it from its string. If he succeeded, his conker became a 'oncer', or a 'twicer', if more than one conker was dispatched. Sometimes the conker was missed and the knuckles were rapped hard. The sudden blow brought howls of pain and tears to the eyes.

When I was nine years old, I was given my heart's desire, the wish I had wished for every Christmas – a pony. She was black with three white socks and a white question-mark on her face. I named her Black Beauty, but Beauty for short. She was a perfect child's pony, and patiently put up with our games, carrying two or more on her broad back. Poems and historical events were re-enacted and, with her help, she became Dick Turpin's Black Bess, or Young Lochinvar's steed ... 'Oh young Lochinvar is come out of the west. Through all the wide borders his steed was the best' (Sir Walter Scott). Or a smuggler's pony ... 'Five and twenty ponies trotting through the dark. Brandy for the Parson, baccy for the Clerk.' (Rudyard Kipling). She stood patiently beneath an oak tree 'for King Charles to land slap on her saddle'. Or cantered round the field carrying Bonny Prince Charlie, disguised as a maid dressed in flowing curtains. She took part in gymkhanas, in sack races, apple in the bucket and bending. Best of all the games with her was hide-and-seek. The seeker would be mounted on Beauty and the last to be found would be the seeker. This game, believe it or not, was played round the Pepper Bros. Timber yard in the evenings. Sometimes the saws would be going inside the sheds where we hid among the stacked timber. Beauty grazed quietly outside the doors, seldom moving far from where we left her with reins hooked around the saddle.

There would be wonderful hiding places among the tree trunks, or behind stacked coffin boards in the old buildings with lofts. I remember so well the paint shed, its wall streaked with dried paint that had been tried on it. The old forge, with its many shoes and nails, was another hiding place, as was, also, the crane which was used to lift heavy tree-trunks. If the chain had been left down, we daringly swung on it, leaping from it on to Beauty's back.

71

We built a lovely ranch house from odd bits of timber, until one evening we arrived to find it gone. Evidently the timber had been needed for some job, and so we were made homeless. In the stables at the timber yard, were the great horses who used to pull the felled trees from the wood to the road. Once the horses would have pulled the timber wagons to the yard, but Pepper Bros. had purchased a steam engine to do most of the hauling. But the horses were used if it was too wet for heavy machinery. Sometimes I was given a ride on one of the horse's back to the stable. They drank from a sunken trough from which the engine drew water, and as they bent their short strong necks to drink, I was always afraid I would slip right down into that deep water.

One day at the farm we unearthed an old set of pram wheels, which were very rusty and minus a wheel. On this frame we fixed a wooden potato tray, made some harness of old bits of string, attached Beauty to it and drove along the farm tracks. Not many yards were traversed before the lopsided conveyance tipped over. Beauty seemed to know when this was about to happen, and stopped. Down would go her head for a quick bite of grass while the wheels were righted. Going down hill we usually bumped into her hindquarters, but never did she kick or attempt to run away. We called that rusty conveyance 'The Golden Chariot'. It remained a long and lasting favourite until, at the outbreak of war, a governess cart was purchased and Beauty was provided with a proper set of harness. We drove her to fetch the shopping or for long quiet drives along the lanes. If we had to visit Ampthill for shopping, or see a film at the Zonita Cinema, Beauty would be stabled at the White Hart Hotel.

I remember one summer day we left home early to visit Aunt Fan, Mother's sister, who lived at Ashwell in Hertfordshire, and Beauty was left to graze in the paddock of The Three Tuns whilst we had lunch. Later in the afternoon we set out for home, arriving back at Priestley late in the evening. Beauty trotted along steadily, and I don't remember that the journey seemed all that long.

Mother had done the journey between Maulden and Biggleswade often enough in the early days of her marriage, stopping the pony and trap at a certain spot to give Alfred, then a baby, his bottle. Now, when I do that same journey by car, it seems a very long way for a little black pony, pulling a Governess cart.

## Shops
Living so far from the village as we did, visits to the shops were few and far between. Mother and Father drove into Bedford on Saturday mornings – Father to market, and Mother to Sainsbury's to buy butter, cooked

tongue, ham, cheese, etc.[1] I can still see, in memory, those men deftly slapping huge chunks of butter into neat pounds and half-pounds. Afterwards we had lunch at the Cadena, where the only thing I would eat was baked beans. As it was a misery for me to be dragged around shops, my Mother deemed it prudent to leave me at home where I was far happier. So my trips to Bedford became few and far between.

Most of our groceries came from Mr Parsons' shop on the square by Flitwick Station, an order being taken over the telephone and the goods delivered to the door. Joints of meat were purchased from Mr Tansley, the butcher, from Ampthill. Each week he would ring through for an order and this, in my younger days, was delivered with the aid of a smart roan cob and trap. And oh, those lovely, plump pork sausages. There has never been a sausage to compare with Tansley's pork sausages. Mr Howlett, the baker from Westoning, delivered fresh crusty bread to the farm every other day. But I can never remember Mother buying cakes from him. Just occasionally, on Saturdays, she bought from Bedford, as a very special treat, a Fuller's walnut sponge cake covered in white icing. There, resplendently cocooned in greaseproof paper, enclosed in a cardboard box, which had the magic words, 'Fuller's Cakes' on the lid, it was placed temptingly in the pantry until Sunday teatime.

Small drapery items were purchased from a shop in Denel End, Flitwick. I came across an old receipted bill, dated Michaelmas Day 1917 ...

> Mrs Cole
> Priestley Farm.
>
> Bought of L Dawson, General Draper,
> and Outfitter – suits to measure.
> Orders promptly attended to.

There is a picture of the back view of a 'sexy-looking' gentleman in a knickerbocker suit, feet well turned outwards. He wears on his head a cap at a jaunty angle, and he carries a walking stick – all most fetching.

---

1  Butter had always been made on the farm by Mother. The bacon and ham produced from the pig she kept in the sty in the yard beyond the back door. But prior to the 1939 War Mother purchased these items from Sainsbury's at Bedford.

Here are the items purchased:

| | | |
|---|---|---|
| Sept. 11 | 4½ tea cloth  9¾ | 3. 8. |
| Dec. 11 | 2 damask  1/9½ | 3. 7. |
| | | 7. 3. |
| | | |
| Feb. 8 | 2 damask  1/9½ | 3. 7. |
| | 4 towels  8¾ | 2.11. |
| | 4 do  1/9½ | 7. 2. |
| | 1 cotton  4½ x 2 wool  2 | 8. ¾ |
| | 3 tea cloth  9¾ | 2. 5. ¼ |
| | | 1. 4. 1. |
| | cloth | 2. 8. ½ |
| | | 1. 6. 9. ½ |
| | discount | 6. ½ |
| | | 1. 6. 3. |

Paid 9/2/18.

It seems that Mother went on a shopping spree in the February! I had to ask Peter, my husband, to check the figures of this bill. Arithmetic was never my strong point. Now I realise decimalisation has made adding up (Father always referred to adding as 'casting' up) that much easier, however much I decried it at the time; those wretched farthings completely floored me.

But the shop we children loved best of all was a little shop opposite the school at Flitwick, kept by a Mrs Britchford, who seemed to me, in those days, very old. One pushed open the door which set the bell clanging, bringing forth Mrs Britchford from an inner sanctum, stepping down into the brick-floored shop. The shop was lined with shelves filled with all kinds of goods. Our nostrils were assailled with the most delightful smells, a mixture of tobacco, soaps, candles, tea and bacon. She also sold string, tins of Brasso, and matches, but what we children liked was the lemonade powder, sweets, chocolates, jars of striped black-and-white bullseyes, gob-stoppers of all colours, slabs of toffee which made your jaws ache with chewing, pink and white nougat (pronounced 'nugget') which could be stretched between the teeth as a bite was taken from the bar, sherbet dabs - sherbet in bags, which could be sucked up through liquorice pipes which clogged and became sodden with sucking - pear drops and many, many more goodies, all so tempting and bewitching. A penny clutched in a hot hand, after long deliberate choosing (which must have driven the poor woman mad), was at last reluctantly passed over the counter in exchange for our choice of sweets, and with cheeks bulging we scampered back along the lane to Priestley. Mrs Britchford, after we had left her shop, returned from whence she came, probably to soothe her nerves with a strong cup of tea, and doubtless muttering out loud her thoughts about 'pesky' children from Priestley.

# Chapter Five

# Rides

As a young girl many happy hours were spent riding my pony to visit the surrounding villages.

## Flitwick

We would set off across the fields to Flitwick, passing the spot where once stood the great beech tree which had been a land-mark and, no doubt, a meeting place for the local inhabitants. We children were told that beneath it ran underground passages from Flitwick Church to Priestley (of course) and on to Westoning Church. However hard I searched I never found a trace of those passages. The beech tree was felled before I was born, so I never saw it in all its glory.

*The old beech tree, which stood on Parsons Hill, Priestley Farm, and was a land mark. This tree was felled by William Baker early in the 1900s. The photograph, believed to be taken by Stanley Norris, shows a group of local lads, probably out for a Sunday stroll. They are, Top Left. Albert Goddard, Albert Chapman, Jack Bunker, John Peat. Bottom Left. Bert Jellis, George Summerfield, George Scott. (Kindly lent by Stanley Peat.)*

I rode into the village along the quiet country lane past the gate to the 'Old Farm' which was once called Little Priestley. Further along the road I would stop and chat with those who lived in the little thatched lodge by the gates which led to Flitwick Manor. Often I would take a bunch of flowers to place on my sister Margaret's grave in the cemetary opposite the lovely old lych-gate of Flitwick parish church. This gate was erected in 1901 by Mrs Aspital, the Vicar's wife, in memory of their three sons who all died in the same year. I would tie my pony, Beauty, to an old wooden gate, which once stood where the lych-gate now stands, and place the flowers beside the stone bird-bath which marked Margaret's grave. Untying Beauty I would continue down Church Hill, which was soft with fallen pine needles from the fir trees lining the road. In summer I would scan the bank for the little sweet wild strawberries that grew there.

On the left-hand side, at the bottom of the hill, standing back from the road, stood the old rectory, where lived William Carr, the blacksmith, with his wife and family, and opposite was a timber and brick cottage in whose barn at one time was kept the church bier. Old cottages, some of

*The old rectory at Flitwick which stood at the bottom of Church Hill, almost opposite the little black gate which led to Flitwick Manor. The Carr family, Flitwick Blacksmiths lived there before it was demolished. (By kind permission of the late Mrs B and the late Miss D Carr.)*

which had thatched roofs, lined each side of the road. In front of the two brick cottages was a low red brick wall over which, in late spring, grew delightful creamy moss roses; lichen also covered the wall, which was warmed by the sun. Childish fingers, mine among them, down the years, delighted to pull off bits of this lichen, much to the annoyance of the inhabitants of the cottages. Not far away was Home Farm built of red brick and timber, with its farm buildings standing behind and to the side. Here I spent many happy hours with Wilfred Abbiss and his son Geoff, who gave me riding lessons and must have got thoroughly fed-up with my haunting them for any spare rides, until my Father finally bought me a pony of my own. Opposite Home Farm was another brick-timber house, once the 'Old Swan Inn'. Here some friends of mine lived, who collected the milk from Priestley each day for their local milk round. Quite often I would be collected with the milk to spend the night with them, returning home the following morning. As I looked out of their upstairs window I thought about the story I had been told of the charity provided by Thomas Deacon in his will dated 11 November 1725, that on St. Thomas's day loaves of bread were to be thrown from the window of the Old Swan Inn for the poor, who would be gathered below. I wonder were there any in that crowd who had made their way over the fields from Priestley to gather up a loaf of bread and, who, perhaps, chanted the old rhyme:

'St. Thomas Gray, St. Thomas Gray

The longest night, the shortest day!'

I could also imagine, as I sat before the fire in the old parlour, the sound of bellringers' voices from the past calling for their pot of ale with which to drink the health of King George at his coronation in 1731 – and paid for by the church!

Beyond the Old Swan Inn was the village green, once the site of the village stocks and pound, with the blacksmith's forge, the pond and the village school where, occasionally, I attended Sunday School, mainly to obtain one of the brightly coloured religious pictures to stick in a book. The idea was to fill the book with pictures (one was given each week) and so obtain a small reward. Alas, many pages of my book remained empty.

Not far from the forge stood the Fir Tree Inn, which stood in twelve acres of land. A tall fir tree grew nearby, from which the inn took its name. The old inn was a fascinating place to me, the oldest part of the building being Tudor, the rest Victorian. (It is such a shame that it is no longer in existence.) I had been told that in medieval times a tannery stood in one of the fields, and many ox shoes were dug up from that site. The garden of the Fir Tree Inn was often used by the artist Sylvester Stannard as a subject for his art students. I would sometimes pass him on my rides, seated at his easel painting some local scene. In those days he

78

lived in a cottage almost opposite the blacksmith's forge at Flitwick. The Stannard family, at one time, lived in Kings Road, Flitwick, having moved from Bedford, and were friends of my husband's family. In their younger days they spent many hours at Thrupp End, Lidlington, where the Roberts' family farmed. There, in the front field, so I was told, were played the fast and furious games of mixed hockey. Harry Stannard, the father, was said to be a good shot with a gun, so he was very popular at the shooting parties which took place at Thrupp End in the early nineteen hundreds.

On my way through Flitwick my Father would sometimes ask me to call with a message for Mr Bunker, the wheelwright, whose premises were almost opposite the school. The yard surrounding the workshop was littered with wheels of all shapes and sizes, some new, some in the process of repair. Inside the shed there was the smell of wood-shavings and paint, and the sound of the tapping hammers and of sawing. Lengths of timber stood against the wall and, nearby, in a corner, a stack of sawn boards waiting to be made into a coffin. Usually my message would refer to a cart needing repair, perhaps some new boards for the bottom of the cart, or a new shaft to make all ship-shape for the coming harvest. The most exciting thing of all was the collecting of a new cart, freshly painted red and blue with *W F Cole* written on the side; this, to me was certainly a 'thing of beauty and a joy forever'. I can't remember there being many new carts, they were built to last in those days, and last they did.

## Steppingley

The farm road which led from Priestley to join the Flitwick-to-Woburn road was made up of hard-packed stones and holes and was always referred to as 'Stoney Road'. By the side of it ran a ditch which, in wet weather, was full of water draining from the land. An old horsekeeper, who frequented one of the Flitwick public houses, sometimes failed, on his ancient bicycle, to make the turn into Stoney Road, and landed in the ditch.

Riding my pony along this road I would make my way to Steppingley, which lay to the east of Priestley, passing the long thick holly hedge, which we believed was the tallest and longest in England. I would take the bridle path which took me beyond Warren Farm Cottages, and on to Steppingley. The lovely old church there is dedicated to St. Laurence, and nearby stands the 'French Horn Inn', where, in later years, before we were married, Peter and I sat with the landlord, Herbert Odell, and his wife, in the their parlour where, whatever the season, on a polished wooden table stood a bowl of freshly-cut flowers. There the talk was of country matters, horses, dogs, sport, flowers and crops.

The woods at Steppingley in springtime are full of bluebells, and that sea of blue stretched far beneath the trees. It was a Sunday evening outing in May for Father to drive out to see the bluebells, with Mother sitting upright beside him, and me protesting in the back; we sallied forth, as my brothers so aptly put it, 'Father, flat out on Ethyl'. (This was an advertisement used for a brand of petrol.) Father drove straight up the middle of the road, stopping suddenly to comment on some crop or cattle in a roadside field. Luckily, in those days, there was very little motor traffic around. I don't think we would have got very far today, with the speed of cars, in the narrow lanes. But, thankfully, Steppingley has its woods of bluebells still.

*Sitting on the running board of Father's car outside the gighouse at Priestley. Perhaps waiting for a trip to the bluebell woods? Evidently prepared for rain!*

## Journey to Hockliffe

At Hockliffe a friend of mine lived at 'Dairy Farm'. The old timbered house stood near to the Watling Street – the old Roman road. When the days lengthened I would ride over to spend a day with her, taking the bridle path that ran by Castle Farm and Daintry Wood, beyond Tingrith. In spring Daintry Wood was full of primroses. The unusual name of 'Daintry' could preserve a trace of the holding of Walter Fitzsimmon, who held lands in Daintry (Daventry).[1] I don't suppose I thought about Daventry as I cantered along the paths lined with curling fronds of bracken, stirrup high. As I passed along the lanes bordered with hedges

---

[1]  A Mower & F M Stenton, 'Place Names of Bedfordshire & Huntingdonshire'.

entwined with pale pink dog roses and wild honeysuckle, the damp wayside ditches were crammed with the lovely scented meadowsweet. Young blackbirds scuttled for safety into the mass of docks and nettles. Sometimes I was lucky enough to espy a nest, with unhatched eggs, and to note their speckled or splodged beauty. We passed on through the little village of Milton Bryan, where Sir Joseph Paxton, the great horticulturist, was born in 1801, and started work as a garden boy in the gardens of Milton Bryan Manor, later moving on to Battlesden House, before entering the service of the Duke of Devonshire, at Chatsworth, where he was working when he designed the Crystal Palace.

Having spent an enjoyable day at Dairy Farm, the pony (it would have been either Ranger or Beauty I chose for the longish ride), well rested after a feed of corn, and I would make our way home, trotting very quickly through Mag's Lane, just in case we met the ghost of Mag, who is supposed to haunt that area of Milton Bryan. We hurried along the headlands of fields of ripening corn, which were turned to a pure gold by the setting sun. The pony, knowing it was on the way home, needed no encouragement to make haste, and we usually sped along Priestley Cover just before dark, scattering feeding rabbits and partridges as we passed.

During my latter years at Priestley the horsekeeper was Ron Peat, who was a good and kind friend. He always made sure, unbeknown to my Father, that the stable and feed were ready for my pony, if I was going to be late home. How welcome it was to see the lamplight shining through the kitchen window, as we clattered into the stable yard. The pony too knew there would be a good feed already waiting in the manger.

## Tingrith

When I rode to Tingrith, the little village that lay beyond the brook from Priestley, I took the road that led past the keeper's lodge, which stands at the top of Clag Hill, (on a map, dated 1890, it is marked Clack Hill). Wide verges line the road and during the Second World War, ammunition was stored in nissen huts along it. It was here that I saw glow-worms sparkling in the dark along its grassy verges and, occasionally, little barking deer, which had escaped from Woburn Park, would bound across the road. The keeper's lodge was built in 1890 for Mr Norris, the Duke of Bedford's keeper. He and his sons were keepers at Priestley until Tom, the youngest, left to join the Royal Air Force in 1941.

Clag Hill ran down to the brook at the turn to Tingrith and Eversholt, a beautiful spot, with the little brook running under the road between grass banks covered with violets in the spring. Woods ran down either side and the brook meandered along the Priestley Cover, dividing it from Tingrith to wind its way to join the Flit, beyond Priestley Farm House. Where the brook passed under the road was a favourite place to paddle, the bed of the stream was sandy and soft for one's toes. Often we would take a picnic and spend many hours there in the pine-scented air, sailing boats of bark, and building dams of stones, giving little thought to the tragedy which had taken place there in the evening of 17 May 1918.

That day had been hot and sultry and, towards late afternoon, a violent thunderstorm broke. For over two hours heavy rain had fallen and parts of Flitwick and surrounding villages were flooded. A travelling seedsman, Mr Leonard Lee, left his home at Marsh Farm, Leagrave (near Luton), driving his pony to a high gig. He was accompanied by a young man, Mr Ted Hull. They were to call on Mr Cecil Browning of Towns End Farm, Steppingley, to do business. When the thunderstorm broke they took shelter for a while, starting out again as the storm passed, and on reaching the bridge at the Tingrith/Flitwick turn, found the road flooded. They were about to turn back when a farm wagon came through the flood. Seeing this, Mr Lee decided to drive his pony on. As he entered the flood water the pony and trap were hit by a great force of water which came from the lake overflowing in Woburn Park. The weight of the flood water accumulating behind the wall brought it crashing down, creating a huge wave of water, which surged down the brook to join with the flood water from the overflowing Tingrith Lake at the very moment Mr Lee was passing. The pony, trap and Mr Lee, who was a cripple and wore leg irons, were swept away. Mr Hull struggled free and managed to cling to some branches. Canadian soldiers, cutting down fir trees at Priestley Cover, rescued him and the pony, which had been caught up in some branches further along the brook. Although a search was made, the body of Mr Lee was not found until 26 May. [1]

Stanley Peat, then a young lad living at Priestley cottages, relates how he was on the spot when they found the body, covered in silt.

'The army was cutting all the pine trees and they were swimming to find him but no luck. We found him some days later, on the Sunday, about two hundred yards from the Tingrith turn. I was there when they found him, it was Jessie Ellis and Mr Sabey, they were dragging the brook.'

Another schoolboy at that time, Mr Farmer (of Ampthill), from Steppingley, was taken by his father to the scene of the accident and remembers seeing the men 'prodding the sides of the brook with iron rods'.

---

[1] A great deal of information was sent to me after I appealed through *The Bedfordshire Times* (October 1987) for details regarding the drowing of Mr Lee. Among the many helpful letters I received were those from Mr L Stewart of Little Staughton, Mr Farmer of Ampthill, (who has since died), Mr Aldridge of Shillington and Mr Day of Maulden, who put me in touch with Mr George Hull, who is the son of Mr Ted Hull, the lad in the trap with Mr Lee at the time of the accident.

The waters from the flooded brook reached the farm, and my brother Alfred, then eight years old, was sitting on the kitchen table catching the boots and shoes as they floated from under the dresser and out of the door. The cottages of the farm were also flooded; the rainwater pouring straight through them from the sloping gardens behind the cottages.

That storm on the afternoon of 17 May broke just as the children were leaving school, and the road to Priestley was long and lonely. Here is an extract from a letter sent to me by Mrs Izzard, who remembers the storm. She was then Cis Peat and lived in one of the farm cottages with her parents, brothers and sister.

'I will tell you a little story about the flood as that is what we called it because I have not known anything like it in my life. It was in the First World War, I was only seven when it ended so I must have been between five and six years old. Do you remember the pretty little thatched lodge[1] at the entrance to the Manor just beyond the church? (It is not there now.) There was a little old lady lived there, Mrs Odell, she used to love to talk to us when we passed to go to school. Well! We were coming home from school one day when a terrible storm broke out as we passed the church, there was only my brother Will and me, and she came out to us and said, "Come in. You will never get home before it gets worse". I think she wanted our company, so we went in and I have never heard thunder and lightening like it, and the rain was like a monsoon. She made some tea and cut up the top of a cottage loaf for us, and we ate it all up. My Mother said we shouldn't have had it as she probably hadn't anything else in the house, she was very poor, but we enjoyed it. After a long time the rain eased up, so we said we had better go as "Mum would be worried about us". I hadn't a coat as it had been a very hot day, so she got out her old black cloak, which old ladies wore, and put it on me. I didn't want it on but didn't like to say. So I kept it on until we got to Long Close. We didn't go the field way home, we went round the road and when we got to the bottom of Parsons Hill, it was just a river, and I dare not go through it as it came above my waist and I cried, but Will grabbed my hand and dragged me through. I was very frightened.'

---

[1] The little thatched lodge, as in the 'Diary of a Bedfordshire Squire', BHRS, vol. 66, p.1, Oct. 1831, the two lodges having been built by a Mr Burrowes.

Coming back to my Tingrith outings, quite often I would leave the pony at home and walk, following a footpath that had been used by generations before me. I would cross the stream by the little plank bridge, where I stood to watch the velvet-coated water voles paddling in and out of their holes in the banks, or scuttling along the bed of the stream, emerging from the water looking quite dry. Here, also, with a small nephew, I fished for tiddlers.

My sister, for a time, lived at Tingrith, opposite the church, with her small son, Ellis. My Father was determined that his grandson should be brought up on the rich milk from Priestley, so, when I walked over to visit her, I would take a can filled with milk from the morning's milking.

The Swan Public House at Tingrith was a popular meeting-place for the men to enjoy a glass of beer and exchange of gossip. Some of the younger men of Priestley and Tingrith walked, or cycled, to Eversholt to play in the village band, which was often hired to play at local functions.

From the top of the church tower there is a good view of Priestley Farm and quite often the village lads would climb the tower to watch for their friends coming across the fields from Priestley. Near the church stood the Manor House where, at Christmas, the children sang carols and were rewarded with mincepies, cakes and money to share. At one time there were five gardeners working in the Manor gardens, producing vegetables and fruit to supply the cooks in the kitchen with enough produce for all the year round.

In the park there was an ice house. These ice houses were the forerunners of our modern refrigerators. They were brick-built, igloo-like buildings underground. Ice was packed into them during the winter, then meat and fish padded in straw were stacked on the shelves or hung from iron rings in the roof. A heavy oak door kept out the air and the food remained fresh until needed.

Some Friday evenings, in the summer, I was allowed to accompany Mrs Smith and her grand-daughter, Elsie, a friend and playmate who lived in one of the cottages on the farm, on a walk across the meadows and over the brook to 'Red Caps' cottages by the road leading from Tingrith to Westoning. There Elsie and I would play outside on the grassy bank while Granny Smith drank a cup of tea in one of the cottages. At last, the long-awaited Mr Bay's white fish and chip van came into view, with its smoking little chimney and chippy smell, making our mouths water. When Granny Smith had made her purchase of fish and chips, and Elsie and I our pen'nth of chips, all tightly wrapped in newspaper, we made our way home to Priestley, stopping at the little plank bridge to drop a few pieces of crunchy greasy chips into the water to see the water change to all colours from the oil.

In Tingrith Park was a lake. In spring, masses of snowdrops grew there and, in winter, when it froze over, it was a place to slide on. One severe winter, a black Shire horse belonging to Mr Bath of Home Farm, fell through the ice into the lake. The horsekeeper at that time was a Scotsman, who, seeing the danger the horse was in, removed his kilt, waded into the icy water, tied a rope around the horse's neck and, with the help of some local lads who had gathered round, pulled the horse to safety. No doubt this story was recounted many times in the public bar of the 'Swan'.

## Toddington

The harness on the farm was kept in repair by a Mr Fox of Toddington. Nothing delighted me more than to be asked by my Father to ride over to Toddington to take or collect some smaller item of harness. I would ride along the road from Tingrith, called Long Lane, which wound along between hedges entwined in wild roses: behind them lay fields of corn or meadows with cattle grazing. The saddler's shop was low and rather dim, and smelt strongly of leather and saddle soap. I can see Mr Fox now in my mind's eye, a rather severe man, with a white moustache. For my twenty-first birthday my Father asked him to make me a bridle for my hunter. It is a lovely piece of work, which I still have in my possession.

Before I set off for home I rode round the village green, where once the Maypole stood and, as always, enjoyed the sign of the public house, 'The Sow and Pigs'. Nearby, I had been told, the legendary W G Grace had played cricket in the 1870s. On our way home we often passed another of Toddington's well-known characters, Edwin Babster. He was a very small man, who visited many of the farms around for eggs, which he carried away in a huge wicker basket.

Along the lane there was a gravel pit, and one hot summer evening some friends and myself decided to go there for a swim. We harnessed Beauty, my pony, to the trap and set off. Arriving at the murky pit, we found other children already there. Beauty was unharnessed and tied up in the shade of a tree whilst we swam. Unfortunately, Beauty slipped free of her halter and made for pastures new through a field of very thistly corn, pursued by us in our bathing costumes. It took us ages to catch her, and we drove home muddy, cross, and very sore.

As a young girl, I helped drive cattle from Priestley to graze in some pastures my Father had rented in Long Lane, near Toddington. I did not realise than that I was following in the footsteps of those people from Priestley who, long ago, had driven cattle to market along that same lane.

Long Lane still leads from Tingrith to Toddington, but it is no longer the quiet peaceful lane wandering between high hedges. Now there is the persistent hum of traffic from the M1 motorway, which runs nearby.

## Westoning

I did not ride very often to the village of Westoning, which lies beyond the River Flit to the east of Priestley. It was quicker to walk and I would take the path across the meadow and cross the Flit by a plank bridge with a very high hand-rail. Although I crossed it often enough, I hated it, especially when I was young and could not reach the hand-rail – the gap seemed enormous!

The River Flit flows along Priestley moor and the Westoning parish boundary; here we picked luscious blackberries in the autumn, and large purple violets in the spring. On Priestley moor grew masses of Heartsease pansies, which I loved to pick and take home for Mother to put in an eggcup filled with water, which she placed on her dressing table.

There was another narrow plank bridge, which led into a spinney on the Westoning estate. This bridge crossed the Flit near the sluice gates, and it was frightening for a child to see the water rushing through the sluice gates below, especially after heavy rain, when there would be a good head of water coming down. It was here, in later years, that my brother gave me my first swimming lesson when the water was not very deep and quite calm, but I, of course, was terrified.

These sluice gates also controlled the flow of water from the junction to the lake in Flitwick Manor. A wide ditch had been dug from the sluice gates, where the Flit and Tingrith brook met; this ditch was known as the 'iron brook' because of the rusty colour of the water. When the water in the lake at the manor dropped below a certain level, Mr Abbiss from Home Farm, Flitwick, would ring my Father at Priestley. The iron handle would be taken from the gighouse, where it was always kept, and the sluice gates lowered to send the water rushing down the ditch and so into the manor lake. This sluice gate was also lowered to drown the hay meadow after the first crop of hay had been taken. This water meadow was the last meadow on the farm before the Flitwick Manor lands. On one side ran the River Flit, and on the other the ditch which carried the water to the manor lake. A small sluice gate controlled the water into the meadow; when this and the main sluice gate were lowered, the water flowed into the meadow, down grassy channels, thus procuring a second crop of hay, and making delightful pools where we loved to paddle and splash. During spring and autumn I would run across the bridge to Westoning in the early morning to gather, for breakfast, horse mushrooms, which grew under the trees in Westoning park. They were the huge flat mushrooms, sometimes as big as dinner plates, whose undersides are very dark; there is no flavour to beat them!

My two brothers, Alfred and Richard, chose their wives from Westoning, and both were married at Westoning Parish Church where, when she was young, Alfred's wife, Irene, played the church organ. Maisie, Richard's wife, attended the church on Sundays, and in the warm spring evenings, when the hedges were thick with sweet-smelling May blossom, Richard would walk across the meadows to meet her from Evensong. Their eldest child, Susan, was christened and confirmed in that old church at Westoning.

*The remains of the sluice gates which, at one time, controlled the flow of water into the water-meadows at Priestley, enabling them to be flooded and so obtain a second crop of grass.*
*(By kind permission of Betty Chambers, Bedfordshire Magazine, vol. 19, no. 151, p. 303.)*

Long ago, the men from the farm cottages would take their boots to be mended by the shoemaker at Westoning. He also put in the hob nails, which strengthened the soles of the boots, to give them more grip. Strong horseshoe-shaped pieces of metal were fitted to the heels, and a metal tip to the toes. A pair of leather boots so made, though heavy to wear, would last a very long time. Occasionally, the boys, full of mischief, would creep up to the cobbler's door in the dusky evening and blow pepper through the letterbox. The cobbler, working by the light of a smokey oil lamp, had his mouth full of tacks ready to hammer into the boot sole. The pepper blown through the letterbox made him sneeze and away would scatter his tacks. By the time he had wiped his streaming eyes and reached the door, the boys would have disappeared and be on their way home to Priestley. I cannot help wondering if the poor man ever swallowed any of his tacks.[1]

During the early 1900s, when Sir Howard Spensley owned Westoning Manor, some Saturday evenings a taxi was hired from Mr Grimmer's garage at Ampthill to collect the maids who worked and lived-in at the Manor, and take them to a dance held at Ampthill. One can imagine the excitement as, beribboned and starched, they climbed into the taxi to be whisked away to an evening of delight and possibly romance. I am quite sure they would have had to be back at the Manor well before midnight, but doubt that any glass slipper was involved.

One Christmas Eve, some carol singers walked from Westoning across the plank bridge to sing carols at Priestley, outside the farmhouse door. Mother and Father were delighted, but my sister and two brothers had other ideas and, for some reason known only to themselves, emptied a jug of water over the singers from a window above. Alas, not surprisingly, in all my Christmases at Priestley there were never any carol singers at Christmas. Country folk have long memories.

Among the men who worked at Priestley two came from Westoning. Mr George Bass walked over the bridge carrying his wicker basket in which reposed his dinner wrapped in a snowy napkin. What delights that basket held; little golden-crusted meat pies from which he deftly carved slices with his 'shut' knife (pocket knife). On the point of the blade he neatly transferred the slice of pie into his mouth. There were wedges of rich plum cake, a chunk of cheese and crusty bread. To us children it was sheer delight to be allowed to peer into the basket's depths to see what mouth-watering goodies it contained.

Joe Walton, the horsekeeper, was another Westoning man. He rode his bicycle over the fields to work. I loved to be around in the dark winter evenings as he finished bedding down and feeding his horses. I would watch, fascinated, as he prepared his bicycle lamp for his journey along the dark bumpy path to the plank bridge. The lamp had a bottom which unscrewed. This was filled with carbide powder, which was well damped; a wick and a small tube led into the reflector. The wick was lit with a match and as soon as the gas coming through the tube caught light, this wick was turned down, leaving a bright white light shining through the glass front in which, on either side, was a small circle of glass which also glowed, green on one side, red on the other. How marvellous I thought this was, but, oh dear, the smell of that carbide trailed behind Joe as he valiantly pedalled off into the darkness.

---

[1] The story of the cobbler was told by Mr Stanley Peat.

## Woburn Sands and Aspley Guise

Sometimes in the summer holidays, or in the early days of autumn, I would saddle up and ride out for the whole day, taking in my pocket sandwiches of marmite or baked beans and hard-boiled eggs. Zipp, my dog, always followed me and seemed to know it was a day out. A favourite ride was to Woburn Sands and Aspley Guise. There, on the sandy soil and dry pine needles, pony, dog and I shared our picnic. I don't remember that it ever rained on such an outing. Now marmite sandwiches always bring back the memory of the scent of sunscorched pine needles. We usually picknicked near the site of the Fuller's Earth works; the deposits of those works have been used for centuries, being added to the water to cleanse the greasy wool shorn from the sheep.

On the journey home, we took the road that leads from Woburn Sands, once called Hog Stye End, to Aspley Guise. There is a very low-lying spot at the bottom of Aspley Hill, which at one time was a very wet area, and a tale is told of a donkey stabled there which died of pneumonia through standing so long with its feet in water. Even I took that with a pinch of salt! Half way up Aspley Hill, on the wall of a house, was a notice telling those in charge of carriages and cart horses to 'loosen their bearing rein'.[1] With thoughts of my favourite book, *Black Beauty* by Anna Sewell who describes the dreadful effects of tight bearing reins with such poignancy, I gave my pony Beauty all the rein she needed. At once she made a dash for a rose overhanging a garden fence and neatly nipped off a bud, which she chewed with relish as we continued up the hill.

## Woburn / Woburn Abbey

During the last war my Father decided I could ride my pony over to Woburn to the estate office, which was situated in the park, to pay the rent due for the farm. This was a wonderful experience for me, as I was allowed to ride along paths that were normally forbidden. With the rent safely in my pocket I set out from Priestley along the cover, which was a strip of land that ran below Priestley plantation, and always held plenty of game for the shooting parties from Woburn Abbey. The Norris family, who lived in the keeper's lodge at the top of Clag Hill, were keepers to the Duke of Bedford and took good care of the woodlands. Priestley plantation was known to hold the best partridge shoot in Bedfordshire.

---

[1] Bearing reins were used on carriage horses to give them an arched neck, mostly for the sake of fashion as it looked smart. A rein ran from the bridle and was fixed to the saddle, the horse could not then put its head down and, although this gave the driver more control over the horse, it prevented it putting its full weight into the collar to pull a load up the hill.

Taking the bridle-path, which led through a wood, I soon came to Woburn park, keeping well clear of the deer so that they were not frightened. I cantered over the velvety turf, towards the Abbey, remembering the Cistercian monks who, for hundreds of years lived peacefully in their isolated Abbey until the 1530s, when their quiet retreat was invaded. The last abbot, Thomas Hobbes, his Prior and one or two of the older monks were brutally hung because they would not accept King Henry VIII as head of the Church of England. The local legend said that they were hung from one of the great oaks near to the Abbey. I hurriedly rode past the trees, and delivered my package.

Before I started for home I rode as far as the two lakes, Great and Little Drakelow, which lie either side of the drive, and made sure that the two lions mounted high on the gateposts had not 'heard the clock strike twelve' and come down from their lofty positions to drink from the lake. I then turned for home, taking the path through the wood which passed a very murky pond, where, at one time, I had firmly believed that if I sat long and still enough I should see a hand appear, clutching King Arthur's sword.

Many of the roads leading from the surrounding villages to Woburn were very beautiful. A leading figure from Kew Gardens used to advise on the planting of hedgerows.[1] I loved to ride along the Woburn to Brickhill road; the hedgerow there was of beech and box, and would glow with rich colour in the autumn sunshine. Nearby villages had cherry, laburnum and large single roses planted on various sites. One of the loveliest times to ride through the park was in May, when the rhododendrons were in flower; they filled each side of the drive with their vibrant colours, set off by dark foliage, and here and there a bush of pure white, or pale pink, flowers.

There were lodges each end of the drive through the park, which were manned by lodge-keepers, who would come out and open the gates for travellers wishing to pass through. During the Second World War, Alsatian dogs were chained by the gates at night to give warning of anyone approaching. There were always animals to see in the park, many kinds of deer lying under the trees, or grazing the rich pastures in front of the Abbey. Towards the end of the First World War bread was delivered to the Abbey from Mr Barnwell's bakery at Pine Grove, Aspley Guise. Mollie Barnwell, (Mrs Guy Humphreys) then a little girl of about three years old, was often taken there in the baker's cart for a ride. Her greatest joy was to see a camel with a white face that was housed in an enclosure quite near to the Abbey. As they approached, the elderly driver of the

---

[1]   Information kindly supplied by Arthur Baynton, Woburn.

baker's cart would say to her, 'Look quick, Mollie B. or the camel will go in and you won't see it!'

Mary, Duchess of Bedford, known as the 'Flying Duchess', built her own hospital – now known as Maryland – at Woburn, where she herself helped to nurse the patients; often she would assist in the operating theatre. After the Duchess disappeared in her aeroplane over the Wash in 1937, a memorial service was held for the tenant farmers. In a newspaper cutting, I found a photograph of the farmers leaving the service; among them, waiting for transport home, are my Mother and Father.

*The tenants of the Duke of Bedford leaving St. Mary's Church, Woburn in 1937 after a memorial service for the Duchess of Bedford who was lost in her plane somewhere over the Wash. My Mother and Father are standing in the front of the picture awaiting transport home.*

I once rode to Woburn to collect an aged grey pony for Mr W Brittain, who farmed Wood Farm, Flitwick, a neighbouring farm to Priestley. Mr Brittain wanted the pony to ride round his flock of sheep. I remember the pony was stabled at the Bedford Arms Hotel, and I was given half a crown (twelve and a half pence) luck money for something that, to me, was a 'labour of love'. However, I spat on the coin for luck, as was the old custom, and no doubt spent the money at the Zonita Cinema, Ampthill.

Priestley's connection with Woburn Abbey and the Russell family – Dukes of Bedford – had begun in 1787, when the Fifth Duke of Bedford bought Priestley Manor from a Miss Egerton. The Russell family took an interest in the different aspects of agriculture. They and their stewards worked to improve the cultivation of cereals, grass and root crops, and to encourage the breeding of better farm livestock. In the nineteenth century they encouraged their stewards and local engineers to design modern farms and agricultural machinery. When the Fifth Duke of Bedford purchased Priestley Manor, here, and in other places, they built new modern farm houses and cottages.

## Godmanchester / Biggleswade / Dunstable

I suppose the farthest visit that I made with my pony was to Offord Hill Farm, Godmanchester, in Huntingdonshire, where my aunt and uncle farmed. I loved to stay with Uncle Bob who, in his younger days, had been a great horseman. One early autumn day I set off from Priestley to spend a few days with them. I followed bridlepaths where I could, passing by the old redundant church at Clophill, and skirting Chicksands Priory. Where I could not follow a bridlepath I took to the wide wayside verges, or jumping a small ditch or two, I would canter across fields of stubble, so cutting down the mileage. The pony and I rested and ate our lunch somewhere near St Neots; from there to Offord Hill Farm seemed to take a very little time.

I rode several times to Biggleswade from Priestley, staying the night at my Grandmother's house, in the Baulk, and taking part in a gymkhana the next day. I also rode with some friends to Dunstable, to swim in the pool there. We took turns to hold the ponies whilst the others swam, returning home with our damp towels and costumes strapped to our saddles.

The old paths and ways were a link with the outside world, and I rode or walked them almost every day, going to school, visiting friends in the villages around, collecting some shopping for Mother, or taking the horses to the blacksmith. I knew and used every bridlepath for miles around, meeting very few people, apart from the keepers and the men and women working in the fields. Thankfully, today, some of the old paths remain and are marked, but what a different countryside! So much is built on, and the great M1 motorway, with its continuously rushing tide of traffic, breaks through the rural countryside, and rubbish is now sometimes strewn where once violets used to grow.

Chapter 6

# Wartime Memories

All down the ages men have left farms and villages to fight for their country or their ideals, and those left behind carried on with the work of the farms as well as they could.

During the Great War, German prisoners were employed at Priestley, being collected each morning from Ampthill in a horse and cart driven by one of the young lads working on the farm. In their lunch break, a large white enamel bucket, containing coffee, was taken out to them and, at the end of their working day, the same lad drove them back to their prison camp at Ampthill.

At the same time, the pine woods lining the Tingrith road were being felled by Canadian soldiers. These timbers were shipped out to France and used to shore up the trenches of the battlefields. News filtered through of the terrible conditions suffered by our soldiers 'over there', and the sight of the telegram boy on his bicycle bearing his sad tidings of 'We regret to inform you...' was dreaded by every household who had a member serving in the forces.

The Second World War saw the arrival of German and Italian prisoners of war, who were employed on the farm when extra labour was required. The Italian prisoners were distinguishable by their brown tunics with yellow patches. The three German prisoners who worked at Priestley, quite regularly, were quiet, hard-working men. One, I believe, had a small farm in Germany and all three seemed thankful to be working in the peaceful fields of Priestley. A lorry, filled with prisoners, called at each farm, leaving the men required and picking them up again in the evening.

Jack Parker who, with his father, ran the milking herd at Priestley, was the first to be called up as he was a member of the Territorial Army. After the war was over, he returned to Priestley for a brief time before moving to Tingrith, where he lived with his wife and daughter. In the little church of Tingrith there is a memorial to him. A wrought-iron flower stand with a brass plate bears the inscription 'Given in Memory of John Francis Parker, 25.4.1907 to 13.11.1979. by his friends at St Nicholas'.

School children had extra holidays from school to help with such jobs as singling (thinning) the sugar beet, which had previously been drilled in rows and stood thickly, waiting to be singled by hand. This left one strong plant at intervals of about twelve inches. Children also helped with the potato harvest, and the picture shows them at work picking up potatoes in Parsons Hill Field.

*School children harvesting potatoes on Parsons Hill, Priestley Farm, during the 1939–45 war. A John Deere tractor, driven by George Lock, pulls the potato spinner, my Brother, Richard, walks at the side. (By kind permission of Bedfordshire Times.)*

During World War Two, twins Jean and Betty Pearson from Birtley, near Newcastle, joined the Women's Land Army (WLA) and were sent to a hostel just outside Wrest Park, Silsoe. They arrived during the summer of 1943; there they were issued with their uniform, which consisted of two green jerseys, two pairs of corduroy breeches, three shirts, one hat, one overcoat, one pair of brown shoes, one pair of black hob-nailed boots, one pair of gumboots (Wellingtons), one pair of leggings, two pairs of dungarees, two smocks, six pairs of knee-length stockings, one oilskin and souwester, and a metal badge, which was a gold sheaf of corn on a green background. The tie had to be bought by the girls. They had an armlet, on which, after six months of satisfactory service, a half-diamond motif was sewn and, after two years' service, a special armlet was issued.

Jean and Betty worked at Priestley for the next three years, working alongside the men, and coping cheerfully with a completely new way of life, doing a variety of jobs around the farm. They would arrive each

*Baver time at Priestley Farm. Jean and Betty Pearson (twins), the land girls from Newcastle, are sitting at the back with George Bass, Eva, another land girl, in front of them. Front row, left. Bert Parker, L Lock, George Lock.*
*(By kind permission of Misses J and B Pearson.)*

morning in a lorry, which called at several farms, leaving land girls at each one. In their tin luncheon boxes were cheese sandwiches, wrapped in muslin. This muslin had to be washed out each night ready for the next morning's sandwiches.

Quite often there would be dances in the hostel at Silsoe, and I would cycle over and join them. Jean and Betty were happy, hard-working girls, and we had some happy times together, though I must admit at first I found their Geordie accent very hard to understand, as I am sure they did my Bedfordshire one.

During the summer months their parents came to Bedfordshire on holiday. They would come to the farm and sit on a grassy bank at the end of the field where Jean and Betty were working, waiting to share their lunch break with them. The hoeing and back-breaking jobs must have seemed endless to them, but they never complained. In 1946 the two girls were chosen to represent the Bedfordshire WLA to present Princess

Elizabeth, now Queen Elizabeth II, with a basket of farm produce. They marched with other members of the Land Army and British and American servicemen to the Bedford Corn Exchange, where the presentation took place. We all felt so very proud of them.

They found Priestley peaceful, even though a war was being fought, and often thought of the monks who, perhaps, had worked those same fields in far-off days. Jean and Betty said, 'The days spent at Priestley were the best days of our lives'.

Priestley owes much to the hard work carried out by these two girls, and we were sad when they left the farm, for home, in the spring of 1946. When they departed my Father gave them a five pound Bond, telling them not to change it unless they had to. My Father summed up our debt of gratitude in a letter he wrote to both of them when they left:

Dated 16 February 1946, and headed Priestley Farm, Flitwick,

'Dear Betty (and Jean)

This letter is to tell you how much I have appreciated your services during the last three years, 1943–1946.

I am very sorry you are leaving, but can quite understand your anxiety to be nearer home.

The work I know has at times been very trying, although I have never heard you complaining.

I hope you will be very happy in the future, but whatever happens, you can feel assured that you did what you could *and did it very well* during the war.

Goodbye Betty (and Jean)

Yours sincerely

WALTER COLE

For all the valuable work and great service to their country given by these and other Land Army Girls, all they were given when the war ended was a pair of shoes, a shirt and a coat. The WLA did not receive a gratuity like members of other forces. During their years at Priestley, Jean and Betty kept a diary, which shows the variety of work carried out by them. They have been kind enough to allow me to print some extracts from this, which can be found at the end of this book. (Appendix 'C')

As petrol was rationed, most of my transport was by horse. I broke both my ponies to harness and did light work with them on the farm, light harrowing for a seed bed, horse hoe and, of course, shopping with pony and trap. Sometimes, on Fridays, I would ride to Ampthill to the bank for Father, leaving the horse at the White Hart Hotel whilst I attended to his business. At other times it was a bicycle, and one had to be careful not to show too much light after dark. Cycling home at night, I would often watch the searchlights criss-crossing the starlit sky, passing the few houses on the road to Priestley, where not a glimmer of light showed through the blackout curtains.

Horses were used by those who had them for all kinds of outings. Some friends of mine drove from Barton to Bedford with a horse and borrowed carriage, to a Ball at the Corn Exchange. The horse was left in a hired stable whilst they whirled around the dance floor and, in the early hours of the morning, rugged up to the eyebrows, it clip-clopped back to Barton.

The mail was delivered to Priestley each morning by Joan Dix riding her horse, whose name, I think, was Lady.

Two little girl evacuees were billeted at Priestley at the beginning of the War. This must have been a dreadful upheaval for them, to be suddenly thrust into a lonely farm house after being used to a busy town life. I don't think they could have been very happy with us, and, looking back, I regret I did not do more to make them feel at home. They were soon moved to a family who lived in Flitwick where they were nearer to the school. I believe they were very happy and stayed until the end of the War.

During the early part of the War, I was at school and so wore school uniform most of the time. Clothing coupons were saved up to buy a pretty dress for some special occasion, and quite often curtain material was used, to good effect, to make clothes.

I remember so vividly one particular September morning during the War. It was misty but warm, promising to be one of those lovely autumn days. We were picking up potatoes in Long Field when, just above our heads, out of the mist, came a Lancaster bomber returning from an air raid. For a fraction of a second one could see the pilot before it crashed into a field a mile or so away. Nothing much remained, but in my mind's eye I see that dreadful moment when those airmen died. Whenever I dig up a root of potatoes and smell that lovely earthy smell, I remember the sound of that crashing plane.

Finally, peace was declared, and some friends and I decided to celebrate VJ night in London. We joined the crowds surrounding Buckingham Palace and got crushed against the railings, from which we were lucky to extract ourselves unscathed. Tired and happy, we then went back to a great-aunt's house in Paddington Green, where we slept soundly on the floor, returning next morning to Flitwick Station and home to face an anticipated peaceful future.

Chapter Seven

# Farewell

## Margaret

Early during the morning of July 24, 1938 my sister, Margaret Billington, died, after giving birth to a daughter who was christened Margaret after her. My parents never really recovered from the shock of losing their beloved elder daughter, and all who knew her mourned her passing. She was very well-known and loved by everyone working on the farm, most of whom she had grown up with. Her body was brought back from the nursing home to lie in the drawing room at Priestley Farm, the home she had loved so much. There, surrounded by masses of flowers, it did not seem possible she was dead, but had simply drifted into a long sleep.

After a service in the packed Flitwick Church, Margaret was laid to rest in the cemetery opposite. My Father describes her resting place in a book he wrote for her two children, Margaret and Ellis:

> Thursday, July 27, and we have laid your dear Mother in Flitwick Parish Churchyard. On one side of the grave is a fence covered with beautiful rambler roses, which I daresay will be moved before you are old enough to read this.

Her memorial is a stone bird-bath, for she loved all creatures. When I last visited her grave my old dog put her paws on the plinth and lapped water from the bowl. I know how Margaret would have loved that.

## Father

The day my Father died in February 1947, the weather was bitter and afterwards heavy snow fell. Father was brought back to lie in the same room as Margaret eight and a half years before.

The days seemed a nightmare, a way of life suddenly shattered, a dear and loved Father no longer there to help or guide. He was laid to rest in Flitwick cemetery. All the morning, wreaths of flowers arrived at the farm, and were taken into the gig house where they covered the floor. The men who worked on the farm lined the path from the lych gate to the Church, the sadness of his passing showing in their faces as he was carried past on the shoulders of the bearers. The turf that covers his grave was taken from the verge of the Great North Road, Biggleswade, where, as a small boy, he was in charge of his father's horses as they grazed on the roadside.

Father was a good farmer and grower. He cultivated his land well. As the old saying goes, 'He put back what he took out', and the land of Priestley certainly knew the farmer's boot.

Our beloved Mother's ashes were buried with him when she died in October 1953.

## Goodbye Priestley and Epilogue

The days leading up to the farm sale remain a blur. I remember the sadness of sorting and packing for Mother and me to move into the little house in Flitwick. A short while before the move, I became ill and had to spend some time in bed, in the same room in which I had been born twenty-two years earlier. There, the men who were leaving the farm came to say goodbye. Implements, harness and tractors stood in sad rows in the field opposite, and I dared not think of the beasts in their stalls waiting the coming of Swaffield & Son, Auctioneers of Ampthill, to sell them off.

On 18 September 1947, at ten-thirty in the morning punctually, my way of living, which I stupidly thought would last forever, came to a close.

Some days later, on a sunny morning, I saddled up Ranger, and, leading Jim and Beauty, followed by my ever-faithful shadow, the little fox-like bitch, Zipp, with a heavy heart I rode away from my beloved Priestley for the last time. Following the old familiar path by the little sandpit, past the ash tree, and on across the fields to Flitwick, I dared not look back at the farmhouse now standing empty. Over thirty years were to pass before I returned.

A few days after the death of my brother, Richard, in 1985, I once again walked the footpath to Priestley. There I found that Mr and Mrs Bonner and their son had a farm shop in the buildings we called the mixing shed. How good it was to hear they, too, loved living on the farm.

Mr and Mrs Little, who now live in the farmhouse, kindly invited me to look over the house, which I found much altered. But some of the rooms still retain that feeling of the warmth I remember so well and I found that, in spite of all the changes that had taken place over the years, it still, in memory, remains the farm of my childhood. My story of Priestley draws to a close, but it is not the end of Priestley Farm, which goes into the future.

# PRIESTLEY FARM, FLITWICK

*Catalogue of the Sale of*

## 24 Head of Cattle

Including 23 Cows in-calf and in-milk, and 1 Shorthorn Bull

## 2 Working Horses

## Agricultural Implements

suitable for a 500-acre Farm

Including 3 Tractors, Tractor Ploughs, Harrows, Rolls,
Binders, Mowers, Cultivators

### Alfa-Laval Milking Machine and Equipment

Dairy Utensils

## Barn Tackle

Including 3 Oil or Electric Engines, Power Mills, Oat Crusher,
Agricultural Carts and Trailers, Harness, Poultry Houses and
Appliances, and numerous other effects

*To be Sold by Auction by*

# SWAFFIELD & SON

(Henry Swaffield — N. B. Foster — L. J. Swaffield)

### On THURSDAY, SEPTEMBER 18th, 1947

at 10.30 in the morning punctually

by direction of the Executor of the late Mr. W. F. Cole.

**May be viewed morning of sale**

Catalogues may be obtained at the Place of Sale or from the
**Auctioneers, Ampthill, Bedford**

C. F. TIMÆUS, PRINTER, BEDFORD

*Front page of the sale catalogue of effects of Priestley Farm.
September 18th 1947.*

*My three beloved horses, outside the barns of Maulden, the day I rode
away from Priestley for the last time. From the left. Black Jim, Ranger,
and Black Beauty. My God-daughter, Susan, is on Beauty.*

To finish, I think my wedding hymn appropriate. On a wonderfully
warm sunny April morning in 1952 Peter and I were married by the
Reverend R Ball in Flitwick Parish Church, the church in which I had
been christened. I drove to church with my elder brother, Alfred, who
was to give me away, and people whom I had known since childhood
came to their garden gates to wave. As we passed the old Blacksmith's
Forge, my dear friend, Rol Carr, left the horse he was shoeing to wave his
hammer in greeting. It was the week after Easter and the Church was still
decorated with lovely spring flowers, daffodils, narcissi and lilies
pervading the old Church with their fragrance. Friends and relatives filled
the pews for the wedding service.

Our reception was held at the Bedford Arms Hotel, Woburn, which
meant we drove along the old familiar road which led past Priestley
Farm, the holly hedge and the Keeper's lodge, where the cherry tree was
a froth of white blossom, and so through the park to Woburn. I have been
among the fortunate ones privileged to live all my life so far in the
beautiful English countryside, surrounded by love.

This is a verse from the hymn we chose for our wedding:

'For the beauty of the earth
For the beauty of the skies,
For the love which from our birth,
Over and around us lies,
Lord of all, to Thee we raise,
This our grateful hymn of praise.'

(Hymns A & M 171, Pierpoint)

## Go the long way
## The long way home

This poem by Sylvia Townsend Warner is from a book of poems given to me in 1946 on my twenty-first birthday by my friend Jean Pepper, now Mrs S Jackson, whose father was one of the Pepper Bros. who owned the wood yard in Flitwick where we used to play. I think it sums up the feeling I had for Priestley when I knew we were to leave there. So many of the things mentioned in the poem were the old familiar things of my childhood. The page in the book is marked with a daisy-chain of dried flowers picked all those years ago from the orchard bank beneath the hedge where the sweet yellow gage plum trees grew.

Go the long way, the long way home.
Over this gate and that lean, at the three lanes' meeting delay,
Look well at that field of hay, eye closely the drilled loam,
Finger the springing corn, count every petal
Of the hedge rose and the guelder rose,
Under the bosom of the blossomed elder stay,
Delay, linger, browse deep on all this green and all this
        growing,
Slant cheek to the sweet air, with deep greeting survey
The full-leaved boughs like water flowing,
The corn-waves hurrying uphill as the wind blows.
Look overhead into the blue, look round,
Watch this bird fly and that bird settle,
With slow treading and sure greet the assuring ground:
Go slowly, for slowly goes this midsummer day,
And this is the last time you will come this way.

Go the long way, the long way home.
Aye, and when you've arrived and the sighing gate falls to
Go slowly, go heedfully your garden through.
Breathe in the spice pinks, turn face up to the soft
Ripe rose that wags aloft,
Nod to the old rake, rub thumb along the spade's edge,
Measure the potato hills and the tall bean rows,
Pledge cherry and currant bush, pledge lily and lily leaf spear
And rebel the nettles waving along the hedge;
Look closely, look well,
See how your garden grows,
Ponder yourself even into the secret cell

Of this year's honeycomb:
Look long, for long has this been yours and long been dear,
And this is the last time you will stand here.

Go the long way, the long way home.
Though you are weary, hasten no ghost to ground,
Tarry this last hour out, take your last look round,
Greet finally the earth, greet leaf and root and stock.
Stand in your last hour poised, like the dandelion clock –
Frail ghost of the gaudy raggle-taggle that you were –
Stand up, O homing phantom, stand up intact and declare
The goodness of earth the greatest good you found,
Ere the wind jolts you, and you vanish like the foam.

SYLVIA TOWNSEND WARNER

(reprinted by kind permission of the Estate of Sylvia
Townsend Warner, the source, and Chatto and Windus as
publishers.)

# PART TWO

# History

*The Flitwick Church dedicated to St. Peter and St. Paul, built in Norman times, probably to replace an earlier Saxon wooden Church. The meadows of Priestley, which lay about a mile west of the Church, provided an endowment for a priest, hence the name Priestley. On the north side of the Church once stood the Priestley Chantry Chapel, built in 1355 by Edmund Bulstrode of 'Presteli'; here a priest was appointed to say mass for the souls of the Bulstrode familty.*

*Through the ages many families have taken the path from Priestley to worship at the lovely old Church of St. Peter and St. Paul, and many rest eternally in its peaceful Churchyard.*

Chapter Eight

# The Earlier Days of Priestley

To me there has always been a magical air about Priestley, my birthplace in Bedfordshire, about two mile south-west of Flitwick. But its history goes back a long, long way further, and a historical chapter therefore seems appropriate. It is bordered on one side by the River Flit, which divides it from the parishes of Westoning, Tingrith and Eversholt. Woburn and Woburn Abbey lie to the west.

There have been many spellings of Priestley. In the Domesday Books of 1086 it is spelt 'Prestelai' and in later documents, 'Prestle', and 'Prestele'. It was probably a Saxon name given to a clearing which was provided to support a priest. Ruxox Farm, which is north-east of Flitwick, became a cell of Dunstable Priory around 1150 and I often wonder if the monks ever farmed this land. Ernest Dix, who was at one time landlord of the Fir Tree Inn at Flitwick, told me a very sad legend about a monk who was working over here at the time of the Dissolution of the Monasteries.

'... this old monk with his small acolyte, a slim lad of some nine summers, came stumbling along the pathway from Priestley carrying their few meagre possessions. They were making for Beadlow, but when they reached the gate by the spinney a man met them and explained that that house had been closed for many years. The monk with the boy in his arms sat in the spinney and sobbed, homeless and friendless ...'

I remember that as a child I was always reluctant to go into the spinney, feeling it was a sad place.

## Priestley Before the Roman Conquest

There is evidence that back in the Stone Age men hunted and fished along the River Flit, where they hunted their prey through the swamp and scrublands that would one day be known as Priestley. Some thousands of years later farmers crossed over from the Continent into Britain and some made their way to the well-drained gravel deposits of the River Flit Valley. No doubt they found at Priestley, lying as it does on the greensand, suitable land for growing their crops and raising their stock.

Not only did one of the old saltways pass nearby but also the ancient road known as the Icknield Way, which joined the Ridgeway in Wiltshire, and thus linked the east coast to the south coast. So the farmers around Priestley had access to overseas trade as well as right across the southern half of England. Eventually metal came into general use in Bedfordshire and long before the Roman invasion, antler horn picks were replaced by metal ploughshares.

### The Romans Come to Priestley

When the Romans arrived, those people already settled in the area of Priestley continued their farming way of life probably benefitting from the new roads built nearby. (I wonder if the farmers grumbled about the loss of land for road building as they do today?)

Ruxox Farm also borders the River Flit and there is archaeological evidence of Roman occupation nearby, with possibly a villa and a temple. The remains of a wharf was uncovered in 1950. At Flitwick a corn drying oven was found which would have been used by the surrounding farmers

*This 'T' shaped drying oven, discovered during excavations at Flitwick was used to dry corn, as do out modern corn driers today. (By kind permission of Kevan Fadden.)*

to prevent their corn from germinating or for turning barley into malt. The local farmers would have been growing barley and wheat and rearing cows, pigs, goats, sheep and chickens and keeping dogs for herding stock and hunting deer. Perhaps they even tried some herbs, and bushes of roses and lavender which were popular at that time. Priestley is not far from Dunstable, which was once the Roman town of Durocobrivis, and no doubt the farmers visited the market. There is no evidence of a watermill at Priestley so maybe they bought querns (millstones used for hand grinding) at Durocobrivis. Whether they visited the Temple at Ruxox, set up a shrine along the bank of the Flit or by some pool nearby, we shall never know. But we can be sure that as they looked out of their homestead they would see the mist rising in the meadows where the cattle grazed among the buttercups, as I did in my childhood.

### Roman Coins Found at Priestley

In 1880 two men, John and Thomas Jellis, were cutting a drain on that part of the farm then known as Priestley Moor, for Mr Duncombe, the occupier of Priestley. Digging deep into the peaty subsoil, one of the men lifted with his spade a lump of what seemed like soil but which, on examination, turned out to be one hundred and seventy-seven coins of Tetricus the Second (AD 268-273). We can only imagine how those coins came to be on that spot. Hoards of coins are believed to have been hidden in troubled times. Other hoards have been discovered in the Flitwick region; Major Cooper, in his report to the Society of Antiquaries in February 1880, mentions other coins being found in an area which, at the time of their loss, would have been swampy and wooded. Perhaps the owner of the coins hid them within the roots of a special tree, or perhaps he was attacked on his way back from some transaction. Although there is no proof of dwellings in that area, perhaps he had a house on some piece of dry ground nearby. If he was attacked, one can imagine his terror, as he let fall his treasure into that murky bog. Maybe he returned to search for it at a later date. We shall never know the true story, or whether the loser was a merchant, farmer, soldier or thief, or just a very frightened man whose worst fears were realised, and who never lived to tell the tale.

### Saxon Settlement

When Britain ceased to be part of the Roman Empire Saxon farmers arrived and found places to settle amongst the native, Romanised Britons. It is the names that they gave their settlements which have been passed down to us. At first they were pagan but gradually the knowledge of Christianity spread back across England. It is possible that a clearing was made amongst the trees so that a wandering priest or hermit could settle and minister to the people of the district. Once the name Priest's ley, or farm, had become established it was quite normal for it to continue despite the many changes that followed.

During the ninth century the Danish raids became more like an invasion and across the eastern side of England many such small estates, which had been intended for the support of Christian priests, reverted to secular ownership. The so-called Dane law boundary passed very near Priestley and when the country became peaceful again many of the mid and north Bedfordshire estates had been divided up into smallholdings for Danish settlers. As the years went by, they intermarried and became absorbed into the local community.

### The New Norman Landlords and the
### Early Owners and Tenants of Priestley

By the time of the 1086 tax assessment, known as the Domesday Book, what had been one farm of around three hundred fertile acres had become nine smallholdings. Each one of these had been farmed by one of King Edward's thanes. The larger part of the Manor of 'Priestelai' had been included in the barony of Nigel d'Albini, of nearby Cainhoe Castle but the new Norman sheriff had retained the smaller part as a form of payment for one of the King's stewards. Albini used his share of Priestley as an estate to support one of his officers, called Thorgils.

We can only guess how the Saxon thanes lived and worked the land at Priestley. If their King called upon them they had to be prepared to leave their farms and follow him to war. I wonder if they watched from the fields of Priestley the Comet, now known as 'Halley's Comet', which appeared in the sky during the Easter of 1066, and wondered, perhaps with fear, what this phenomenon could mean. They would have known of the death, in January, of Edward the Confessor and that Earl Harold, Godwinson, had been crowned King. Perhaps some of them followed him to York in early September and with him celebrated the victory over the Norwegians. If those left at home to gather in the harvest, heard about the landing of William of Normandy they probably thought it was too far away to affect them. Some of the thanes and their men from Priestley may have marched to that battlefield near Hastings where the history of England was changed, where William won the throne of England and hundreds of Norman officers won themselves the right to own estates in England. It is possible that on that blood-soaked turf at Battle, before a Norman arrow found its mark, one man's last thoughts were of cattle peacefully feeding beside the River Flit at Priestley.

The land at Priestley which was reserved for the King's steward was a useful mixed farm which was worked for him by an agricultural labourer. Thorgil's farm was also mixed and we can imagine the sixteen plough oxen grazing down by the River Flit and the forty pigs grunting and snuffling as they buried their unringed snouts deep into the oak leaves below the trees of the spinney. Living around the farmhouse was a full time agricultural labourer and four other men who possibly looked after the pigs and worked in the woodland.[1] I wonder if their children got up early, as I used to do, and followed the men out into the woods and fields, returning later with pockets full of mushrooms or hazel nuts, and hands full of flowers?

We do not know what happened to the thanes but those who survived the battlefields of York and Hastings may well have found themselves working their own land for the new Norman landlords. Although they were so far from the battlefields the farmers of Flitwick, including Priestley, suffered very badly during the winter of 1066. Duke William's troops crossed the country, living off the land and they left Priestley, which had been worth £3 in such a bad way that it was revalued at £1. Twenty years later it still had not recovered.[2]

The Albini family, of Cainhoe Castle, were one of the main landholders in Bedfordshire and despite the fact that as the years went by, in the absence of a male heir, their estates were divided between daughters, Cainhoe and its surroundings stayed with various branches of the family until it was bought by the Grey family of Wrest Park (Silsoe) in 1428. The list of their tenant farmers has not survived but Thorgils, their Domesday tenant, also held the Manor of Tingrith from them, and after his death the two manors continued to be let together. The position is confused because of the division of the Priestley Estate at 1066. It appears that in the mid thirteenth to the mid fourteenth centuries, the Hospital of St. John of Jerusalem, whose local headquarters were at Melchbourne, had an interest in Priestley.[3] Maybe it was the smaller part which had once been farmed by the King's steward?

## The Priestley Chantry Chapel

Several families are mentioned in connection with Priestley but the most interesting are the Bulstrode family who may have connections with the wealthy family who owned land in Bushey and Watford. In 1355 Edmund Bulstrode of 'Presteli' built a chantry chapel in the churchyard of Flitwick which was consecrated in honour of the Blessed Virgin Mary and St. George. Walter Richere was the first priest; he was appointed to say masses for the souls of Edmund, his wife Matilda and son, another Edmund. When Edmund Senior died, Matilda continued to appoint priests, as did the next family to own the chapel but the last recorded appointment is 1393. There is no mention of the Priestley chantry when

---

[1, 2]  Domesday Book, Bedfordshire, ed. John Morris, published by Phillimore.
[3]  Victoria County History, Bedfordshire (VCH Beds.) vol. 3.

*Photograph of Church showing site where Chantry Chapel is believed to have stood.*
*(By Nigel Baldock, by kind permission of Reverend Roy Hubbard.)*

PRIESTLEY CHANTRY CHAPEL

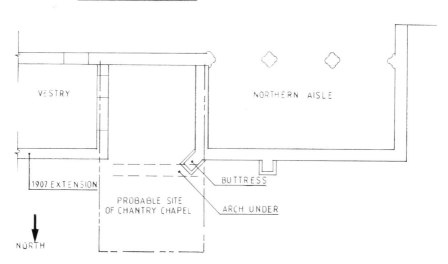

VESTRY

NORTHERN AISLE

1907 EXTENSION

PROBABLE SITE
OF CHANTRY CHAPEL

BUTTRESS

ARCH UNDER

NORTH

*A plan of Priestley Chantry Chapel at the Church of St. Peter and St. Paul, Flitwick.*
*(Plan drawn by Nigel Baldock.)*

112

they were officially dissolved in the reign of Edward VI. Some later owner must have let the chantry lapse. However, the chapel remained although it does not seem to have had any further connection with Priestley. In 1555, the Vicar of St. Peter and St. Paul, which is thought to have been built on the site of the little Saxon church served by the original tenants of Priestley, was the Rev. John Collop. As Flitwick church had been administered by the Prior of the Augustinian Priory at Dunstable, he may well be the John Collop who had lost his position in that town when their Fraternity was closed down. The Collop familiy appear to have had influence in the area and to have regretted the passing of the old ways. In 1587 Reginald Collop stated in his will that he wished to be buried 'within the chapel lying unto the chancel and Parish Church of Flitwick'. Also, that his son, his executor, should give 6s. 8d. (33⅓p) 'towards the repair of the chapel adjoining the Church of Flitwick for the space of 20 years'.[1]

It is probable that after the Collop family support finished, the chapel quickly fell into decay and ruins, as nothing now remains. In the Diary of a Bedfordshire Squire, 1794-1858, John Thomas Brooks of Flitwick often refers to ruins, which were close to the Manor House.[2] I wonder if these could have been the remains of the Priestley Chantry Chapel? We can now identify the site of the chapel because when the north aisle was built in 1857, by William Butterfield, it was not possible to extend it as far eastwards as intended because a large vault of coffins was discovered. Also, in 1907, when the vestry was enlarged, foundations of some former buildings were found on the outside of the vault, which coincide with the vault of the Priestley Chantry Chapel.

Little is known of the Priests who chanted the masses and of the souls for whom the masses were said in that candlelit quiet building. Perhaps if you stood quietly by the north wall of Flitwick Church on a late warm summer evening, when the scent of the few pine trees lining Church Hill fills the air, (that is, if there are any quiet moments with the houses so near) you will feel the whisper of those Holy Prayers.

When, as a family, we attended Flitwick Church, the Harvest Festival comes to mind. In our Sunday best, Mother, Father and I left Priestley and made our way to Flitwick Church. Father led the way to the Priestley pew which was situated by the wall on the north side of the Church, and there we knelt, as those from Priestley all those centuries before had knelt, though I did not know it at the time, and though we prayed in a different tongue, we prayed to the same God and for the same reasons, no

---

[1]   'The Story of an Old Bedfordshire Village', p. 124-5, Rev. J L Ward Petley
[2]   BHRS, vol. 66.

doubt, as they had through their priests, for the saving of our souls, for those we loved, and for the land we loved.

## King Henry VIII Takes an Interest In Priestley

The Grey family manor house was at Wrest Park, Silsoe. The family had lived there since the thirteenth century and despite various changes of fortune did not finally sell the estate until the Second World War. The nearest that the family came to losing Wrest was during the lifetime of Richard, third Earl of Kent, who was not only a heavy gambler but also lived an extravagant life at court. His son, Sir Henry Grey, was obliged to buy what would normally have been his inheritance. Because of his efforts to revive the family fortune he allowed the title to lay dormant and concentrated on improving the estate. He enlarged the park by taking in land from Flitton and Clophill.[1] King Henry VIII was also enlarging his Bedfordshire parks and in 1540 he exchanged, with Sir Henry, land at Priestley for Gravenhurst.

His interest in Priestley was mainly the valuable grazing which lay so temptingly near the royal parks at Steppingley and Beckerings. He was also interested in the rabbit warren. Back in the early fourteenth century, William de la Marche had obtained a charter of free-warren at Priestley. Rabbits were a valuable asset to the estate and were carefully protected by a warrener.

The farm and warren were originally included with the property which had come to the Crown at the Dissolution of the Monasteries and were managed by the Officers of the Court of Augmentation, at Ampthill.[2] The warren was let to Simon Lowen, together with grazing on the farm for five cows and one horse and enough grass to make six cartloads of hay. The rent was £16 per year. However, King Henry or his steward then decided to take back two-thirds of the warren and enclose it within the Royal Park at Steppingley, leaving a disappointed Simon Lowen with a piece, which, together with his hay and grazing, was only worth £6 per year.

It was the same with the grassland. The piece called Cowle(y) was let to George Acworth of the Moat House, Biscot (near Luton), the fields known as Pypers and Dames to William London, and the rest of the fields were shared between William Style, Nicholas Hopkyns and John Leper. Their combined rents were intended to be £24.13s.8d. (£24.68 1.2p) but by the time that Henry had taken a large acreage for each of his two parks, the remaining tenants only paid £5.25p) between them.[3] The

---

[1]   'History of Bedfordshire', Joyce Godber
[2].   BHRS, vol. 64, pages 43–45.
[3]   BHRS, vol. 64, pages 317–319.

following year (1543) what had become known at Priestley Park was transferred to the care of Sir Francis Bryan.[1] For some years he had been steward to the Lordship of Ampthill and Custodian of the Great and Small 'Ampthill Parks'. As King Henry made regular visits to hunt at Ampthill Park, he may well have ridden across the fields of Priestley.

However, Queen Elizabeth took less interest in her Bedfordshire estates and in 1560 she sold Priestley to Richard Champion of London and John Thompson of Husborne Crawley, along with land at Lidlington and the rectory of Marston Mortayne.[2] Thompson was at one time sheriff of Bedfordshire.[2] He died in 1597 and his helmet rests on the canopy of his red-veined alabaster tomb in the north aisle of the Church of St. James and St. Mary Magdalene, Husborne Crawley.

It is likely that it was Champion who, in 1703, sold Priestley to a member of the Cuthbert family. Jeffrey's map of 1765 marks Priestley as 'Sheldon's Farm'. As in 1704 the parish register records the birth of Cuthbert, son of Gustavus Sheldon and his wife Elizabeth, it may well have been bought for the young couple by Elizabeth's father. Three more of their babies were baptized at Flitwick Church in the next five years. Cuthbert grew up to marry and inherit the Manor of Priestley. The burial of his wife, Sarah, is recorded in the Flitwick Parish Register on 24 May 1746, and his own burial 2 January 1765. They do not have children entered in the Flitwick register, but maybe they were baptized at Elizabeth's home church, as Priestley was not sold for more than twenty years after his death.

## Priestley Becomes Part of the Bedford Estate

In 1787 Priestley was bought by Francis, fifth Duke of Bedford, and another phase of its history had begun. In *Flitwick – A Short History*, the Ampthill Archaeological Society have noted that on a map of 1798 – 'The Duke of Bedford owned the ancient manor of "Prisley" divided into Wood Farm, Warren Farm and Priestley. Little Priestley, now "The Lodge", was a farm owned by the squire' (of Flitwick). They went on to explain that these farms were, '— old enclosures of arable and pasture land centred around their farmhouses and away from the main village'.[3]

So Priestley Farm had now become separated from the woods and warren which had been so precious to King Henry VIII. In 1804 the Bedford Estate Office let the valuable agricultural land to the Duke of Manchester, of Kimbolton Castle. He paid £184.2s.9d. (£184.13½p) for the first year's rent after which it was increased to include the water

---

[1, 2]  VCH Beds, vol. 3
[3]  'Flitwick, The Story of an Old Bedfordshire Village', p.25, Rev. J L Ward Petley.

meadows.[1] After the death of the Duke of Manchester, the Kimbolton steward continued managing Priestley for his executors. By 1809 the estate policy was changing and one of their bailiffs took over the management of Priestley Farm and ran it with help from a resident foreman.

Andrew Wilson is recorded as bailiff in September 1809 and then in April 1817 Thomas Todd took over. He is probably the Thomas Todd, who, in 1824, described the roundsmen system (see below) in Husborne Crawley and Eversholt, to a Select Committee on labourers' wages; in which case he was living in Woburn.[2] He was followed as bailiff by Joseph and then William Todd. In April 1835 Charles Burness became Bailiff.[3]

This was a very difficult time for farmers and farm workers alike. There was very high unemployment and the only financial relief came from the Poor Rates. The hated roundsmen system, whereby unemployed labourers were forced to do a 'round' of all the farms in the parish, offering themselves at a very low wage, which would later be topped up out of the Poor Rate, was in use in Flitwick.

### Riot at Priestley

On December 6th, 1830, the farm workers of Flitwick got together and discussed ways of persuading farmers to give fixed employment to as many men as possible, and at a living wage. They marched from farm to farm and forced the men working there to go with them. A few days later Edward Crocker, steward of the Bedford Estate, (Woburn), wrote to the London steward to explain what happened as a result of this meeting.[4] One group, carrying sticks, shouting and sounding very threatening, arrived at the gates of Priestley Farm. Holland, the foreman, kept his head and went out to meet them, before they entered the farmyard. He asked them what they wanted and they explained that they were looking for local men who had received money to be sworn in as special constables and who might be used to force them back to work. He talked to them quietly and rationally and pointed out that if they caused violence they might be transported or even hung. One by one they threw down their sticks and grumbling amongst themselves, walked back towards the village. Trouble had been averted. Outside the gate and back along the road, Holland picked up thirty-eight sticks!

---

[1]   Bedford County Record Office Disbursements 1804.
[2.]  BHRS, vol. 60, pages 61-62.
[3]   BCRO Establishment Finance Subsidiary ACC, Ref. 5/1480, Russell Estate Archives.
[4.]  BCRO R3/3571 quoted in BHRS, vol. 57, pages 101-2.

The men should have been very grateful to this calm and sensible man. They got back into the village just before the arrival of a strong group of constables but there was no violence. When shortly afterwards, Lord Grantham, the Lord-Lieutenant, arrived they explained to him that they had no intention of causing a riot but only wanted to demonstrate that they couldn't live on their present wages. From among the crowd, which was later estimated to have been over a hundred, only four were arrested. They were accused of threatening Mr Cardale, the unpopular magistrate, from Lidlington. On 4th January 1831, they were taken before the magistrate at the Quarter Sessions. Three of them were let off with fourteen days' imprisonment but the fourth, who had previously taken the money to be a constable, received six months'.[1]

Throughout these troubled times the Duke of Bedford, through his agents, worked to get a minimum wage of ten shillings (fifty pence) per week. Wherever possible he provided allotments and encouraged his tenant farmers to do the same. Gradually conditions improved, the countryside became peaceful once more and the Duke of Bedford continued to make improvements for both farmers and farm workers.

## A New Farmhouse for Priestley

Sometime within the ten years that followed the riot, the Duke of Bedford ordered a new farmhouse to be built at Priestley. At the time of the 1841 census Alexander Mitchell, age thirty-five, bailiff, is recorded as living there with his twenty-five year old wife, Mary. However, the estate policy changed soon afterwards, and in 1847 Henry Platt was offered a tenancy. In the 1851 census Henry is recorded as being twenty-nine years old, his wife Elizabeth was twenty-three and their two daughters, Frances Susan and Harriet Elizabeth, were aged one year and one month old. Living with them was Henry's unmarried brother, aged twenty-four. He is described as 'fund holder'. The two children were registered as having been born at Flitwick and were probably the first babies to be born in the new farmhouse. The Platt brothers had been born at Lidlington.

The Platts stayed at Priestley for at least another twenty years and with help from the census records we can follow the growth of their family and their changed circumstances. In 1851 they were employing twenty-five labourers on the farm and an eighteen year old youth – (Charles Smith of Little Brickhill) as groom. He lived in the farmhouse and there were three resident domestic servants, Jane Beeson, unmarried, age twenty-five from Weston Turville and two teenage girls. On the night of the census there was also a labourer's wife, called Martha Bead,

---

[1]  QSM 30, pages 185–6. Quoted in BHRS, vol. 57, pages 101–2.

staying there. She was thirty-nine years old and originally came from Biggleswade.

Ten years later the farm is described as three hundred and eight six acres but, having been there for about fourteen years, Henry Platt had probably changed his system of farming; he had cut his outdoor staff to fourteen men and six boys. There had also been changes inside the farmhouse. The two little girls had now been provided with a governess, Augusta Clibusion, a thirty-one year old, unmarried lady from St. George's Parish, London. There was an eight year old brother, Henry Edward, who possibly joined them in the schoolroom. The family also included a four year old brother, Charles Frederick and a little sister, two year old Emily Mary. The domestic servants had changed; they now employed twenty-three year old Elizabeth Swain, from Calverston (Bucks), as cook/house servant, and twenty-two year old Eliza Woodford from Gawcott (Bucks) as a general servant.

By 1871 the farm policy had changed once more. Perhaps encouraged by the example of his landlord, the Duke of Bedford, Henry Platt was not only employing thirteen men but also seven boys. They now had a total of seven children. The first two girls were in their twenties, Henry Edward was eighteen, the two middle children were fourteen and twelve and had been joined by nine year old Arthur and eight year old Elizabeth. The governess had gone; a National (Church of England) School had opened at Flitwick in 1852 but it is probable that the Platt children were going to a private school. The indoor servants had changed once more and Mrs Platt was employing Ruth Whittington from Flitwick and Emma Bowden from Leicestershire.

When the detailed census opened in 1841[1], there was only one cottage at Priestley Farm. Crowded into it was Edward 'Hollit' (Hollet) aged forty, his thirty-six year old wife Sarah, their nine children, ranging from one week to age seventeen, and a fifty-five year old lady, Mary Phillips, described as nurse. It is probable that she was there to care for Mary and her baby. This last child died during her fourth year and was buried in Flitwick church but there is no record of the burial of Mr and Mrs Hollet in the Parish Register. However, when in 1840, Mr Pearce, the Vicar of Westoning, had wanted the Duke of Bedford to help him financially, to build a schoolroom, he explained that the children from Priestley Farm, who attended his Sunday School, were Dissenters but that their parents had asked if they could attend his new school when it was built.[2] Thomas Bennett, the Duke's steward, pointed out that the Duke was only

---

[1]  Public Record Office, Kew (Census 1841-1881).
[3]  BHRS, vol. 60, pages 150-160.

*This picture was found with one of Priestley Farm House among my late parents' belongings. It is believed to be the old Priestley Farm cottage, probably lived in by the Hollet family before the Duke of Bedford rebuilt new cottages in 1856.*

proprietor of one cottage at Flitwick, that at Priestley.[1] It is, therefore possible that Mr and Mrs Hollet were buried in a Nonconformist graveyard. There was a Baptist Sunday School in Westoning but the Hollets obviously preferred Mr Pearce's Sunday School. Mr Pearce made it clear to the Duke's steward that once he had a day school, he would not force the children of Dissenters to attend the Sunday School. It is of interest that in 1844, Her Majesty's Inspector reported that although the Westoning Schoolmaster, who was under the direct supervision of the vicar was 'active and intelligent', he could do more for the religious instruction of the children.[2] Despite financial difficulties the school continued to get good reports and if the young Hollets did attend this school they obviously got a good basic education. This may account for the fact that during the winter of 1848, the older boys applied for an assisted passage to Australia. The above Mr Pearce also ran a small private school at Westoning; he was a personal friend of the 'Squire' of

---

[1]   BHRS, vol. 60, p. 160-161, - the Duke contributed £20.
[2].  BHRS, vol. 67, p.91.

Flitwick, John Thomas Brooks and tutor to his young sons. Mr Brooks kept a detailed diary in which he recorded his visits to Mr and Mrs Platt at Priestley Farm and also to the Hollets' cottage.[1] On Thursday, 21 December 1848, he attended a meeting of the Parish Vestry to discuss the '— emigration of the young Hollets'. The members of the church committee were not enthusiastic when asked to take money from the poor rates to send poor boys to Australia. However, Brooks wasn't discouraged and walked out to Priestley to discuss the subject with the Hollet family. A fortnight after the first meeting he attended another meeting which was held in Flitwick church. This time the rate payers agreed to raise part of the money to send some of the unemployed people from Flitwick to 'Port Phillip' (now Victoria). After the meeting he gathered those who were about to emigrate together in the church and gave them a few words of advice.[2] He continued to visit the Hollets during the weeks of waiting. He never named the people who emigrated nor do the Ampthill Poor Law Committee, who on January 18th, 1849 set aside £75 towards their expenses.[3] By the time of the 1851 census, Edward and Sarah Hollet had only got two of their original nine children living at home, Charles who was fifteen and Thomas twelve, but they now also had Martha aged seven and Henry aged five. Of the older children, Mary, now twenty-seven, Elizabeth twenty-two and Ruth fourteen had left home, possibly into service. Elizabeth returned to be married in Flitwick church, September 1847. John twenty-five, George twenty, and William eighteen had also left home and they were probably the 'young Hollets' about whose emigration Mr Brooks had been so concerned.

Ten years later Edward Hollet was still working for Mr Platt and is described on the census form as 'widower'. Martha, who was supporting herself by plaiting straw, and Henry, who was working on the farm, were still living at home. In 1871 Edward, now aged 72 was living with Henry, his wife and five year old son.

In 1856 the Woburn Estate Office arranged for two new farm cottages to be built at Priestley. It is probable that the Hollets moved into one and John Richardson and family into the other. By 1861 the latter had three sons and three daughters, ranging from six to sixteen. Also sharing their cottage was Mary Cain, aged eighty, probably Sarah's widowed mother.

---

[1]   BHRS, vol. 66, ed. Mr R S Morgan, by kind permission of Mr J C Lyall.
[2].  BHRS, vol. 66, p. 112.
[3]   Beds. CRO.

Richardson, Peddar, Cain; these are all familiar Flitwick names I remember from my childhood. Some of the families who lived at Priestley, during the nineteenth century were there for more than forty years. How well they must have known every tree and meadow, every field and pond. Like me, they must have known just where to find the first mushrooms and blackberries. When the young Hollet girls left their family and went away to work among strangers and the boys paused in the labours as they worked on an Australian farm, did they think back to the days when they played around the old farm buildings of Priestley, listened for the first cuckoo and waded in the brook, looking for fish and taking home armfuls of bright kingcups?

## Rural Industries : Straw Plait and Lacemaking

Although the men living in the Priestley farm cottages were fairly sure of a permanent job all the time they were active and healthy, others in Flitwick were not so lucky. Also, as we have seen, some of the agricultural workers had large families and at times wages were very low. In common with many of the other women and girls of Bedfordshire, their wives and daughters earned extra money by plaiting straw, sewing hats or lace making. In 1851, Mary Whittington, of Warren Farm, was listed as a straw plaiter but she was adaptable and by 1861 she had found she could make more money as a lacemaker, while her two daughters, who were still living at home, aged forty-two and twenty-nine, were both straw plaiters. Also, in 1881, Samuel Whittington's daughter-in-law at Priestley, and three granddaughters were all entered in the census as straw plaiters. Many other examples could be quoted and we can imagine Mr Bunker, the Flitwick plait dealer, driving up the farm road in his pony and cart to collect their finished work. No doubt the ladies and older children used a brass 'splitter' which divided the coarse straw into narrow strips. Plaiting these fine pieces of straw was far more difficult but the fine plait was sold at a premium. Behind the door, or crewed up beside the chimney, would have been a plait mill, a small wooden mangle which flattened the plait when it was finished. Joe Peddar's wife, Lucy, was entered in 1881 as a hat sewer. The railway station opened in Flitwick during 1868 and from then on many of the women and girls travelled daily to work in the Luton hat factories. During the eighteen eighties the manufacture of felt hats gradually began to take over from straw. The waste from the felts was called 'shoddy', and truck loads were sent to Flitwick station for use on the farms. Father would send his horses and waggons from Priestley to collect it and would then spread it on the land as a manure.

Mary Whittington is the only one of the Priestley ladies who was recorded as a lacemaker. This was probably because, to get the best prices for lace, it was necessary to live on or near the route of a lace dealer who would bring the cotton and patterns and collect the lace made to order. Down in the village there would have been many ladies making lace. A dear elderly friend on mine remembers, as a little girl, having to do so

*This delicate Bedfordshire pillow lace was worked for me by Mary Pressland of Flitwick, whose mother, as a girl, had to do so many heads of lace before she was allowed out to play. Twenty-four pairs of bobbins were used to make this piece. (Kindly photographed by Nikki Kedge.)*

many heads of lace before she was allowed out to play. (A head is the edge or peak of lace). During the warm summer evenings, the women would sit in the doorways of their cottages, with their pillow, busy at their lace, their fingers nimbly flying among the pins and bobbins as they chattered to neighbours or those passing by who stopped for a few words. When I was a child I loved to sit with 'Granny Smith' outside her cottage door at Priestley in the sunshine. She had white hair swept into a bun at the nape of her neck, her face, with speedwell-blue eyes, was as rosy as an apple and her little black and white, silky-coated dog, Nell, sat at her feet. There was the scent of the sun-warmed box-hedge which surrounded the garden as she worked away at her pillow lace, with bobbins weighted with their seven different coloured glass spangles (beads) sparking like cut gems. Such joy when she allowed me to weave a few of those bobbins and so make that lovely delicate tracery of thread that is typical of Bedfordshire lace. This childhood experience helps to make me a link in the chain which makes up the fascinating history of Priestley.

## More Changes at Priestley

Sometime before 1880 the Platt family left Priestley Farm and during the next few years there were several changes. First of all thirty-five year old John Duncombe moved in. He was unmarried and employed thirty-five year old Martha Millard, from Cranfield as housekeeper and sixteen year old Sarah Barnes of Flitwick as domestic servant. He was running Priestley Farm with fourteen men and three boys and was running it together with Warren Farm. The new keeper's cottage, which stands at the top of Clag Hill, now known as Flitwick lodge, was kept in hand by the Bedfordshire Estate Office.

In 1900 Stanley Harris took over the tenancy and in 1902, Sydney Street from Great Farm, Maulden, took over, together with C E Phillips. Street's father used to breed Oxford Down sheep, which he sent out to South America. When Sydney Street left Priestly, he farmed at Brogborough Manor.[1]

My father-to-be, W F Cole, with his wife, Eva, son Alfred, and daughter Margaret, moved from Hillcot, New Road, Maulden to Priestley Farm in 1914. He took over a rather smaller acreage – (229 acres) – which he ran with twenty men and boys. He remained at Priestley until his death in 1947. The Duke of Bedford, through his Estate Office, then decided to lease the farm to Bedfordshire County Council who divided the land into eight smallholdings.[2] During the next twelve months the Council had the

---

[1] 'Information kindly supplied by the late Miss M Street, of Cranfield.
[2] Bedfordshire County Record Office, AOC 23/4/1/1-18.

farmhouse divided into two dwellings and modernised the two cottages. The tenants of the land, cottages and two farmhouses were:

| | Acreage | Tenants |
|---|---|---|
| No. 1. Part house & buildings | 72.269 | K H & E S Westrope (Pulloxhill) |
| No. 2. Part house & buildings | 60.395 | H A & J Olney (Westoning) |
| No. 3. Cottage pt. buildings | 23.118 | E Bonner (Flitwick) |
| No. 4. Cottage pt. building | 23.118 | A W & A Carr (Flitwick) |
| No. 5 Land | 14.051 | A Brinkler (Westoning) |
| No. 6. Land | 14.051 | H R Bunker |
| No. 7. Land | 12.472 | F Turner (Maulden) |
| No. 8. Land | 8.531 | A Brinkler (Westoning) |

In 1955, Priestley Farm was sold by the Bedford Estate to Bedfordshire County Council. Now, in 1991, the farm house remains as two dwellings, the tenants, Mr and Mrs G Little, having both; they farm 110 acres, milking a herd of ninety pedigree Jersey cows, with twenty-four heifers of between one and two years, and thirty calves under one year. They retail thick Jersey cream of the most delicious flavour. Part of the house they let to visitors as a self-catering holiday home.

The two farm cottages were converted into one home in 1972 by Bedfordshire County Council. Mr and Mrs E Bonner, who live there, are the only original tenants of the Beds. CC and, with their son, Mark, now farm one hundred acres. They also run a farm shop where one can purchase the very best of fresh fruit and vegetables, also flowers and plants from a large greenhouse which now stands where once were boiled up the pig potatoes.

Both the Little and Bonner families feel a great bond with Priestley and its past. I know it is in good hands. How fortunate I am that, when I visit my old home, I am shown so much kindness.

*NOTE:* I am deeply grateful to Vivienne Evans for her help in sorting out and pulling together my historical notes.

# PART THREE

# Appendices

*This watercolour of stooks of corn on Priestley Farm was painted by my sister, Margaret, in her teens, at a time when she was one of the students of H J Sylvester Stannard.*

# APPENDICES 'A' and 'B'

# From the Ledgers of Walter Cole, 1941–1946

These extracts are from my Father's farm ledgers, given to me after my brother, Richard, died.

A list of work to be carried out in each field was left in the office at Priestley, for the benefit of my brother Richard, who took charge when Father was away from the farm, (Appendix 'A').

There is also reference to a day's work carried out on the farm, plus a list of seed and corn prices, and the charge for ploughing etc., as quite often contract work was done for other farms from Priestley, (Appendix 'B').

# Appendix 'A'

# Work Carried Out at Priestley

## 1941-1946

### Long Field

Plough up Brussels stalks. Cut off long stalks if sticking up. Alf King with two horses would do it best.

Plough ready for peas. Lay stalks in furrows.

Get sugar beet (seed) in as soon as possible after scuffling both ways.

Don't drill too thick or too deep. Won't matter about a few clots (clods) for sugar beet and mangolds.

Harrow in and roll with light flat roll if still dry.

Harrow then flat roll this end (Farm end) so that you get a crop of weeds up before setting marrows.

Parsnips. Hand roll crossways and planet hoe, as soon as possible also primo cabbage.

Try hand roll up Brussels plants (rows) then hoe.

### Pond Field

Get cocoa bean waste and spread cavings. Plough as deep as possible. May want discing opposite pond. Roll or harrow. 'Stitch out' and plant King Edward potatoes.

### 11 Acres

Disc well both ways after liming or after a nice rain.

### 7 Acres

Wheat, harrow when damp with two horses weight harrows if necessary.

Broccoli and Kale land. Scuffle stalks both ways with John Deere (Tractor) stalks will then pull up, and dry up.

Plant with Majestic (potatoes) seeds.

Chop the Kale down. All that Parker (Cowman) will not want. If in flower just chop the flower off for cows.

## Parsons Hill

Finish ploughing, when finished potato setting, or when too wet to plough anywhere else.

## 15 Acres

Tractor harrow two sets up and down by side of Oats. Then harrow all crossways. Not Oats. If it pulls up use horses, then roll field right across. When dry, ought to be done before end of April.

## Holly Hedge Field

Set potatoes as soon as possible. Plant about 20 inches apart. Cover well, if tractor won't do it have Alf and Ron with horses.

## Cover Hill

Drill the grass seed both ways where there isn't any. harrow in with horses. Cut the seed in a little so that it loosens the weeds. Would then flat roll it if dry.

## Round the Cover

Wheat ground. Don't think I would do anything with it unless you think it would be best light rolled to fill mole holes in. Don't smother the small seeds, leave till well up if you do, roll it.

Oats. I think it would do them good to roll crossways with the small heavy horse roll, a little later, would do best when dry after a little more rain to soften the clods.

Barley. Biggest pieces of turf might be picked up and laid in heaps on the grass, so that it can be put back when next ploughed. Also rolled crossways with the heavy tractor roll, but turn on the grass.

Rye. Would do good to harrow with horses crossways then roll crossways with light roll.

## Water Meadows

Sow 2cwt salt. 2cwt ammonia to acre and harrow again. Also the moors ought to be done first week in April.

## 1942-1943

## Moors

When rushes have finished spread 1cwt dried blood, 1cwt ammonia mixed with 2 or 3cwt lime to acre. Then harrow or disc harrow. (Note: Cover Hill was first ploughed up during the First World War

(1914-1918). In 1941 grassland (The Covers) was ploughed up by order of the Bedfordshire War Agricultural Committee.)

In 1943, on Friday 12 March, there was a white frost and the ground very hard. The Army were on manoeuvres and had arrived at Priestley. Soldiers were everywhere, camping in barns and kitchen. Father was not too pleased as, contrary to his advice, they had driven a tank straight across the fields and over the brook, where they had become well and truly stuck.

The next entry in the book contains this address.

Claims Officer
Eastern Command, Home Forces,

with a copy of the bill for damages, with, I might add 'paid' written against it.

| | |
|---|---|
| Fencing round drinking place | 1. 0. 0 |
| Post to Water Meadow | 1. 0. 0. |
| Post to Water Meadow | 1. 0. 0. |
| 4 posts and fence horse paddock | 1.10. 0. |
| Filling holes in 4 men 4 hrs. | 1. 4. 0. |
| Filling holes in 1 man 3 hrs. | 4. 6. |
| | £5.18. 6 |

## 1941

### A Day's Work

Tues. Aug. 19 1941. Heavy dew. Light shower, fine and bright for rest of day.

Alf King harrowed and marked out leek ground. G. Lock and Alf King after breakfast cutting at Mrs Collins. R. Peat. Parker, Joy, Odell, setting out beet. Geo. Scott, T. Chapman, J. Oakley setting out beet. Geo. Bass. C. Oakley packing marrows. Shocking Rye and Wheat. Rolph and H. Atkins horseshoe in 13 acres until 11 o'clock. Then H. Atkins horse drag Holly Hedge Field and Cover Hill. B. Bridgestock and Son horse hoe Kale.

After tea Rolph and H. Atkins T. Parker, Bridgestock mowing round oats.

Jim Jeeves load from farm. B'Wade to London.

# Appendix 'B'

# Prices and Crops

| | 1941-42 | 1943-44 | 1945-46 |
|---|---|---|---|
| | ton | ton | ton |
| Potatoes | King Edward £8 Seed | Doon Star £8.53 Scotch Seed | Majestic £12.10 Set Seed |
| | Majestic seed, £7.5 once grown | King Edward £10.10 Seed | King Edward £12. Scotch seed |
| Peas bag | 2/6 July 9/- | | |
| Peas seed | 100/- cwt. Onward | 129/- cwt Superb | Meteor Early Bird, 151/- cwt. |
| Sprouts | | Dec. £28/ ton | |
| Parsnips | £8 ton | | £8.10 ton |
| Parsley | £11-£13.10 | | |
| | £18 ton | £20 ton | |
| Onion Seed | | 32/- lb | 30/- lb |
| Cabbage Seed | 12/- lb. Primo | | 14/6d lb. Primo |
| Carrots | £6.10 ton | | |
| Mustard Seed | 160/- cwt | | |
| Barley Seed | | 180/- seed qr. | 145/- qr. |
| Wheat Seed | | | 102/6d qtr. Yeoman |
| Oats Seed | 60/- qrt. | | 90/- qrt. |
| Mangolds from pit | 40/- | | |
| Lettuce Seed | | | 10/6d |
| Straw | 3/6d truss | | 3/6d truss |
| Bags | | 9d each 6d | 1/- |
| Parsley Seed | | | 5/- lb. |
| Corn Cutting acre | 21/6d. 30/- oats | 18/- | 25/- |

| | **1941–42** | **1943–44** | **1945–46** |
|---|---|---|---|
| Ploughing acre | 27/6d to £1 (Tractor) | | |
| Allowance to Ploughman | 6d acre | | |
| Harrowing | 5/- | | |
| Scuffling 'acre' | 10/- | | |
| Disc Rolling | 5/- Disc, 3/6d rolling | | |
| Drilling | 7/6 | | 7/6 |
| Drilling peas | | 1 horse  2 horses | |
| | | 6/-d per hr.  7/6 per hr. | |
| Stitching potatoes acre | 7/6d | | |
| Tractor driver week | | £6 | |

| | **1934/35/36** | **ton** | **1937/38** | **ton** | **1939/40** | **ton** |
|---|---|---|---|---|---|---|
| Potatoes | King Edward Seed | £4.15 | Doon Star Seed | £6 | King Edward Seed | £6 |
| | Doon Star Seed | £7.10 | Majestic Seed Seed | £7 | King Edward | 7/- cwt |
| | | | | | Majestic once grown | £6.10ton |
| Peas bag | 4/-, 3/-, 5/-, 3.6d, 10/- | | July 7/6 | | 6/6d | |
| Peas Seed | Thomas Laxton 50/- cwt | | | | | |
| Brussels Sprouts | March 1/6 bag | | | | | |
| Onions | £4.10 ton £6 ton | | | | | |
| Cabbage Seed | | | | | | |
| Wheat Seed | | | 36/- qtr. | | | |
| Oats Seeds | | | | | 55/- qtr | |
| Clover Seeds | | | | | 224/- cwt | |

| | **1934/35/36** | **1937/38** | **1945/46** |
|---|---|---|---|
| Bags (Hessian) | | 3d | |
| Ploughing | | | 25/-, 15/-, 17/6, £1 acre |
| Labouring | W. 4/6 day, Man 6/- | | setting out beet 1/1 hr. men Stalk digging 9 hrs. 7/6. |

# Appendix 'C'

# From a Women's Land Army Diary 1943–1946

Joan and Betty Pearson, the land girls who worked at Priestly during 1943 and 1946, returned home to Birtley, near Newcastle, Co. Durham. I still correspond with them, and a few years ago they returned to Bedfordshire and we all visited Priestley Farm, a visit bringing back many memories. They have kindly permitted me to use these typical extracts from the diary they kept during their three years at Priestley Farm, which they always say were among the happiest days of their lives.

### January

We went out topping. In other words we had to take the tops out of Brussels sprouts, it would be freezing cold, you had to flick the snow off to find the tops.

Putting cabbage stalks in the furrows to be ploughed in for fertilizer.

If wet outside, sorting onions in the loft where they had been stored until required.

Cleaning mangolds,

Cleaning beetroot,

Putting up potatoes from the potato pit, potatoes were stored under straw and covered with soil in the Autumn ready for use. Someone shovelled potatoes into a machine, someone else turned the handle and the potatoes came up a conveyor belt for sorting.

### February

Digging leeks if ground not too hard.

Weeding parsley.

Dung flinging from the heaps already on field. Turning dung from one side of a narrow yard to the other. A job we did not like doing, as we smelt dreadful. The girls wouldn't sit next to us going back in the truck because we smelt so awful.

Harrowing with horses, after a field had been ploughed. This was done to break up the soil.

## March

Weeding parsley. Cleaning beet, pulling rhubarb, preparing ground for sowing onion seed. The onion bed was prepared by pulling a large roller over the ground. Sowing fertilizer ready for setting potatoes. Planting cabbage plants, a back-breaking job. Planet hoeing peas. A planet hoe was an implement with long handles attached to a wheel fixed between two blades. This was pushed along the rows to cut out the weeds.

## April

Hoeing cabbage, pulling rhubarb, digging up parsnips, still leek digging. Sowing fertilizer ready for potatoes.

## May

Singling out beetroot, setting Brussel sprouts, cutting cabbage and parsley.

## June

Picking peas, crawling along rows of beet thinning them out, setting leeks.

## July

Stooking corn, weeding onions and parsley. Threshing oats.

## August

Setting kale plants, pitching corn, stooking corn. Pulling onions.

## September

Spreading shoddy[1] over the fields ready to be ploughed in.
Pulling onions, picking beans, cutting lettuce, bunching parsley.

## October

Topping sprouts. Digging sugarbeet (chopping off the tops with a sharp curved knife, one hand was held behind your back in case you chopped off a hand by mistake). Cutting cabbages. Gleaning potatoes, (picking up into a basket, all potatoes left on the ground by the potato digger).

## November

Flinging dung over the field ready to be ploughed in.
Picking tops of Brussels sprouts.

## December

Picking sprouts. Plucking fowls.
Other jobs during the year would be stone picking (cleaning a piece of land to be ploughed of the larger stones. These would be carried in baskets to the headland, where later they would be used to fill in the deep ruts in the cart tracks of the farm).

---

[1]  Shoddy was pressed waste fibre sent down from London in trucks by rail.

# From the Nature Notes of Mrs R D Cox (née C M Dix), 1930-1934

This record of Flora and Fauna seen at Priestley was sent to me by Mrs Ronald D Cox, (née C M Dix) and known always as 'Dicky'

Dicky was born at Flitwick and was brought up to love and appreciate the beauty of nature all around her. She loved to be in the woods and fields, and, from an early age, was encouraged by her parents and relations in her special interest in wild flowers, their country names, and the folklore surrounding them.

She was educated at Luton High School for Girls, and was hoping to read history or botany at university but, unfortunately, this ambition was not fulfilled, and she left Flitwick in 1934 to take up a career in nursing, passing her S.R.N. finals in 1938 at Bedford County Hospital. In 1940, Dicky married Ronald Cox, an accountant. After the war they settled in St. Neots, Huntingdonshire, (now Cambridgeshire) where Bernadette, their daughter, was born, and she has carried on the family tradition of country life and read agriculture at the University of Newcastle, receiving her Honours Degree in 1968. Dicky now has five grandchildren. Ronald, sadly, died in 1980.

The records of flowers and birds and butterflies kept by Dicky during her school days and just after, from around 1930 to 1934, were based on lanes and fields on, or near, Priestley Farm. The notes are remarkable, partly because they are the work of a young girl, partly in reminding us of the proliferation of species visible in such a small area in those days - would it be anywhere near the same nowadays? They bring back a picture of the countryside, when one could wander quietly along the roadside and hedges. All these delights were to be found on and around Priestley as I grew up. I remember especially the kingcups, great golden chalices glowing in the marshy places. Each season brought its own delight. Finding the first flower to bloom in spring was like finding hidden treasure. The ditches in summer were crammed with meadowsweet, and who has not tried to hold still a frond of quaking grass?

One of my earliest memories is of being held upside down in a field of cowslips and asked, "What can you see"? With petticoats over my head, and no doubt knickers showing, I had to answer, "London Town", whereupon I was set the right way up.

I feel very fortunate that Dicky has given me permission to include these delightful records of her collections in my book of Priestley. I hope they will give you reading them as much pleasure as they gave me.

# Appendix 'D'

# Butterflies

| Month | | Description, eggs, habitat etc. | Place or plant where seen |
|-------|---|--------------------------------|---------------------------|
| June | *Red Admiral* | Single eggs laid on nettle leaf. Caterpillar or larvae hatch from June onwards. Fasten leave edges to make a shelter in which to pupate. Few hibernate, majority migrate south for winter | Stinging netttles, back of building |
| | *Common Blue* | Greenish eggs laid on rest harrow or bird's foot trefoil – two lots between May and September. Second brood larva hibernate at base of plant and pupate in April – pupae mainly green. These butterflies congregate in the evening and nest together clinging to long grass, head down | Roadside hedgerow opposite crab |
| July | *Painted Lady* | Single egg usually laid on thistle; the larvae feed in silk webs on the leaves, then pupate inside leaves made into shelter with silk. Fly July and August, migrate south, very few hibernate in buildings | Thistle by cornfield track |
| | *Wall Brown* | Can resemble the fritillary. Greenish eggs laid on grass. The larvae feed on this grass by night. Two generations. First flies May or June. Second flies July or August. Hibernates where it can find shelter. | Roadside near entrance to farm |
| | *Peacock* | Olive green eggs laid in large clusters on nettles. Black "spiny" larvae. Feed voraciously, and grow together in a silky web until July when they separate into the undergrowth. Pupae grey green or even brown with two horns on the head. Hibernate in buildings hollow trees or any crevice | Shed |

| | | | |
|---|---|---|---|
| | *Large White* | Yellow eggs laid in very large groups on any cabbage-like plant. The larvae are greedy and smell awful. They pupate on walls, fences and suchlike. The pupae are greenish grey with black spots, attached to fence by a silk pad or belt. Two generations May-June and August (should be killed on sight!!!). They overwinter as pupae, butterfly emerges in April | Nasturtium near garden fence |
| August | *Marbled White* | White eggs dropped at random in the grass. On hatching the larvae eats the eggshell, then hibernates until early Spring – pupae creamy, speckled brown, faintly pink in places. Butterfly emerges around July | Tall grass, edge of meadow probably for hay |
| September | *Meadow Brown* | Yellow eggs laid in the grass. Larvae over winter The pupae are green but the wing cases are outlined in dark brown. The pupae attach themselves by a long thread to grass stem. Butterflies emerge Spring | Pasture |
| | *Small Tortoise-shell* | Eggs laid in clusters on nettle leaves, the larvae are tiny and black. They feed on the leaves within a silken web – two lots. June and August to September. Butterflies usually hibernate in buildings from the end of October | Nettles above ditch near farm |

# Moths

| | | | |
|---|---|---|---|
| April | *The Streamer* | Moths fly in the evening along the hedges. They lay their eggs on the wild rose; usually stem or buds, on which the larvae feed. They pupate in June and July | Caterpillars on Dog Rose in hedge near plantation |
| May | *Narrow-Bordered Bee Hawk Moth* | Day flying – resemble bumblebee (protection from predators). Wings are often transparent (scale lost during first flight). Eggs laid under leaves of food plant, larvae feed in June, July. Pupae overwinter inside coarse but silky cocoons which lie on the earth just covered with earth and debris. The moths usually fly "mornings only" in May and June. They hover over scabious, lousewort, bugle etc. | Devil's bit Scabious by wayside |

| | | | |
|---|---|---|---|
| | Cinnabar 'Mother' Moth | Occasionally fly-lazylike – during day, but usually seen at dusk. Garishly coloured, black, orangey, red. Shiny yellow eggs, larvae not very hairy, but very greedy. They will completely denude the ragwort of its foliage. They are very flamboyant in colour, yellow barred, and never still. The dark brown pupae overwinter just underneath the soil or dead leaves. Moths fly May and June | Ragwort by plantation |
| June | Red Chestnut | Whitey-yellowish eggs laid in batches on dock, dandelion or groundsel. The larvae are strong, dark brown in colour. They pupate just below ground. Moths emerge about April | Caterpillars on dandelion field edge |
| | Heart & Dart | Has black markings on wings and thorax. Its white eggs have purple markings and are laid on turnip and other vegetable leaves. Larvae hatch July and August, pupate in underground cells, and complete growth the following Spring | Cultivated field |
| | Turnip Moth | White eggs are laid in batches near stems of food plant from which the larvae feed from July to October. Larvae hibernate during winter, pupate underground in the Spring. Moths fly June and July | Cultivated field |
| | Burnet Companion | Flies by day. Green eggs laid in batches on clover, larvae feed by night. The pupae hibernate in ground in cocoons of silk and pieces of plant | Hayfield |
| | Mother Shipton | Markings on front wings look like a wizened old witch. Flies by day. Dull green eggs laid in clusters on clover, larvae feed from July to September. Chestnut brown in colour, white powdery, overwinter in silk cocoons attached to grass | Clover patch |
| July | White Ermine | Flies at dusk and by night, late May and June, July. It has a number of black spots on white wings. Lays white eggs in large numbers under dandelions, docks, etc. Larvae are plump and very hairy, about September they make cocoons of silk and their own hair, and overwinter in the litter on the ground | Docks near path on way to Westoning |

| | | | |
|---|---|---|---|
| | *The* | Pale eggs are laid on sowthistle, lettuce etc. | Daytime |
| | *Shark* | Larvae feed by night from July to September. | resting on |
| | | The brown pupae make cocoons of earth, | tree trunk |
| | | and the moths emerge from the soil in June | |
| | | or July. They fly by night | |
| August | *Green* | Greenish moth whose caterpillars move | Hedgerow |
| | *Carpet* | with a hump movement. It flies at dusk in | opposite |
| | | the hedgerow. Larvae feed chiefly on | crabs |
| | | bedstraws. Overwinter as larvae | |
| | *The* | Brown-like (house mouse colour and | Hedgerow |
| | *Mouse* | scuttles when disturbed in much the same | opposite |
| | | way). Its dark coloured eggs laid usually | Holly hedge |
| | | on hawthorn, where they overwinter. | |
| | | The larvae feed on the leaves from | |
| | | April to June, but pupate in the soil | |
| | | until moths emerge July and August | |

*Note:*    There are several more that could fly at Priestley, e.g. Oak-eggar moth in the wood. These have speckled yellow wings and lay their eggs on woodsage, wound wort and dead nettles.

| | |
|---|---|
| Moths are usually night flyers | Butterflies never do |
| Moths' wings fold over the body | Butterflies fold their wings upright above body |
| Moths have straightish antennae | Butterflies have small knobs at the tips of their antennae |

# Insects

| | | | |
|---|---|---|---|
| March | *Crowd of* | The larvae are legged grey grubs. | Hibernating |
| | *Seven* | They hunt the aphids etc. over the | in crevice of |
| | *Spot* | foliage just like the adults. The pupae | tree trunk |
| | *Ladybirds* | hang by the tail to leaves. Ladybirds | |
| | | are weather prophets and fortune-tellers. | |
| | | They are known as the little birds of | |
| | | the Virgin Mary | |
| | *Sloe Bug* | Feeds on flowers and berries. If in short | Sloe bushes |
| | | supply they feed on wheat | on roadside |
| | | | opposite |
| | | | plantation |

GALLS

| | | | |
|---|---|---|---|
| | *Robin's* | 'Cynipoidea' very small minute parasites | Dogrose |
| | *Pincushion* | – difficult to see. The "galls" mature in May | in hedge |

| | | | |
|---|---|---|---|
| | *Oak* *Apple* *Galls* | Globe shaped galls, mature into brown 'apples'. The wingless females lay eggs in the oak roots, making root galls – flat brown pancake looking, lying on top of each other like brown crockery stored away. The females from these climb the oak and deposit their eggs in the shoots to form oak apples and start the cycle again. The males have wings and fly | Stunted oak in hedgerow by road |
| | *Spangle* *Galls* | Gall wasps lay their eggs in the veins of oak leaves, lentil shaped galls appear on the leaves in August. The mature ones are red. The grubs overwinter in the gall – pupate there – and emerge in April as adults. All female. These gall wasps deposit their eggs on the oak tree flower stems and the grubs form 'currants' on the stems and leaves in May and June. Male and female wasps emerge from these | Stunted oak in hedgerow by road |
| May | *Hawthorn* *Shieldbug* | Principal food hawthorn berries or oak leaves, overwinters as adults, only one generation in a year | Hedge by roadside |
| | *Holly* *Leaf* *Miner* | Lives in the holly April, May and June. The eggs are laid on the underside of the mid rib close to the base of the leaves. The larvae feed on the leaves from September to May even during severe frost. They pupate in the leaf. The larvae make yellowish blotches and lines edged with brown on the leaves | Holly hedge |
| | *Bark* *Beetle* | Woodboring beetle lays its eggs underneath the bark, the galleries that the adult and larvae make look like Egyptian hieroglyphics. They fly in April, May and again in July, August | Elm on pathside |
| | *Violet Ground Beetle* | | Farm track |
| | *Ichneu-* *mans* | Predator on the large white butterfly caterpillars | Near farmhouse |
| June | *Lacewings* | Four green filmy wings and "soul destroying" golden eyes. Don't be misled, they look fragile but are savage predators. Feed on aphids etc. Hibernate during winter | Path to Westoning |

| | | | |
|---|---|---|---|
| | *Grass-hopper* | Can fly only very short distances. A 'hop crawl'. Its song is made by rubbing the hind femora against closed wings. Feeds on surrounding vegetation | Barn at back of Spinney |
| | *'Cuckoo-Spit'* (Frog-hopper) | A thin skinned insect frog like in jumping ability, also in appearance. Covers itself with froth so that it doesn't dry up. Lays its eggs in splits in dead stems late October and November | Long grass – hedge bottom |
| | *Crane Fly* (Daddy longlegs) | Its larvae is the destructive leather jacket. It lays small black eggs at plant root in the soil. The larvae feed all through the winter, and pupate in the soil | Spinney gate |
| | *Leaf Cutter Ant* | Carrying its piece of leaf | Roadside near retired policeman's plot |
| July | *Click Beetle* Rain Beetle* | This beetle propels itself from danger by suddenly reflexing its abdomen, and in so doing makes a loud 'click'. The larvae is the destructive wireworm. But even so, you must not step on or kill the parent, if you do – it will rain! | Farm track |
| | *Drone Fly* | Looks rather like a bee. Its white eggs are laid near a manure or suchlike heap. The larvae move into the fluid to pupate. They winter in any hollow place | Farm track |
| August | *Horsefly* or *Clegs* or *Dung-flies* or *Gadfly* | The females are notorious bloodgetters during dampish thundery midsummer weather. Very much so when humans are near. Warning note is a hum. The male lives on nectar. Eggs laid in dampish places | Meadow near bridge over brook |
| | *Solitary Bee* | Emerging from its sand hole | Back of spinney |
| | *Hover Fly* | Eggs long and white. Larvae are blind but they eat aphids. The fly migrates for the winter | Farm front gate |
| | *Devil's Coach-horse* | This is the beetle in which the devil hides himself and eats the bodies of sinful men! When it bends its back over its body it is cursing you! It was | Cultivated field |

the only insect to enter Christ's tomb after the crucifiction. It usually hides under a stone all day. Both beetle and larvae are very fierce and will bite

| | | |
|---|---|---|
| *Bumble Bee* | Clumsy honey bee with buff tail. Only young fertilized queens survive the winter, hibernating in a hole. The colonies are always an annual event | Meadows |
| *Wood-wasp* | Swift flyer. Rose leaves rolled up with silk make homes for larvae, each one lives on its own | Farm front garden |
| *Stag Beetle* | Long-lived and nocturnal; found with its larvae | Rotten branch of wood |
| *Dung Beetle* or *Cockchafer* or *Dumble-Don* or *Lousy Watchman* | Lives on cowpats. Has a lazy evening flight | Meadow |

## SNAILS SEEN, OR SHELLS PICKED UP

Common snail, known as Wallfish

Garden snail

Small white snail

After a heavy August thunderstorm the bank down to the farm was covered with large far horned black slugs. One or two orange ones around the post

## SPIDERS

Garden spider

Harvestman

Gossamer spider – autumn 1932 over the stubble field, and part of a hedge the spiders had spread the loveliest of gossamer webs. Name gossamer drived from 'goose-summer' or Michaelmas

# Animals

| March | *Toad* | quite puffed by roadside ditch |
|---|---|---|
| April | *Grey Squirrel* | rushing across the road from Blundell's Long Close to the spinney |
| | *Hedgehog* | laboriously trundling across track late evening |
| | *Stoat* | hunting in and out of the hedgerow, swift sinuously and menacing |
| May | *Grass Snake* | green and quite lovely in meadow grass |

| June | *Field Mouse* | sometimes called yellownecked lives on seeds, fruit, snails and insects |
|---|---|---|
| August | *Harvest Mouse* | shy – noticed in corn late afternoon |
| | *Shrew* | seen on path bank, early evening. Lives on earthworms, etc. Has to eat three-quarters own weight daily |
| | *Longtailed Fieldmouse* | or wood mouse – edge track by plantation. Eats seeds, berries, shoots, snails etc., can climb trees and often uses old birds' nests to store food, and also as a dining room to eat in |
| | *Bank Vole* | very shy creature, feeds on fruits, seeds and nuts. Seen late afternoon |

# BIRDS

| *Pheasant –* | cock and hen |
|---|---|
| *Blackbird* | |
| *Hedge Sparrow's* | nest with sky-blue eggs |
| *Hedge sparrow –* | often called dunnock – very shy, keeps to thickets, feeds on insects in ground litter |
| *Chiffchaff Warbler* | song "Chiff-chaff", sings from top of tallest tree |
| *Ring Dove* or *Wood Pigeon* | soft lullaby coo – nests in tree fork, only lays two eggs |
| *Tree Creeper* | |
| *Cuckoo* | |
| *Missel Thrush* | sings "How d'ye do – How d'ye do – Bopeep – Bopeep" |
| *Yellow Hammer* | sings "Little bit of bread and no cheese" |
| *Greenfinch* | song descending scale of notes – choo-ce-o |
| *Jay* | broken scream |
| *Wren* | |
| *Water Wagtail* | very shy bird |

I would think that you had swallows or maybe house martins with the brook so near. My lark is recorded from the ridgeway, and my robin from home – the kingfisher from the "river" Flit's tributary in the Westoning Road spinney. There was a kingfisher there for several years until someone dug in the bank, and it went.

144

# Appendix 'E'

# Trees and Shrubs

## March

| | | |
|---|---|---|
| *Blackthorn*<br>*Whitethorn*<br>Sloe | Flowers arrive before the leaves, when in full bloom a cold spell for a few days (Blackthorn Winter). Boughs made into walking sticks, bark is a febrifuge, leaves used to adulterate beer. Berries made into sloe wine – tasted rather like an inferior port. | Side of road opposite plantation |

## April

| | | |
|---|---|---|
| *Elderberry*<br>Dwarf elderberry<br>grows more south<br>is known as<br>Danewort | Planted by wayside to keep off witches. Flowers made an ointment, berries a winter cordial (Elderberry wine). Its pithy wood makes popguns for boys, skewers for butchers, and the old yeomen their finest arrows. | By farm building |
| *Wayfaring Tree* | Leaves and berries powerfully astringent. Berries make ink, the leaves mixed with alum make a yellow dye and rind from the root makes birdlime. | Hedge by road |
| *Hawthorn*<br>May | Insignia of the Tudors. The crown of Richard III was found in a hawthorn bush after the battle of Bosworth Field. It was Mary Queen of Scots' favourite tree. | Hedge |
| *Crab* | Apples make crab apple jelly. Wood burns with a lovely scent. | Hedge by road |
| *Larch* | Red flowerlets, small, lightcolour cones. Deciduous fir.<br>A fungi, called Golden Boletus favours the neighbourhood of larch from summer to late autumn. I looked for years but never found one It is edible, lovely smell, lurid to look at – yellow – flesh turns red or violet ring around golden stem. | The Spinney |

145

| | | |
|---|---|---|
| *Wild Cherry* | Wood used to make walking sticks and pipes. | On the roadside just before the Gamekeeper's Cottage |
| *Holly* | White flowers in April-May. Protective plant against evil. | Highest hedge in England Roadside |
| *Mullien* Aaron's Rod. Flannel. High taper, Hag taper | The Romans dipped the stems in tallow and burnt them at funerals. Used to light candles on the alter (taper). Ointment from flower used in chest complaints. | Cobbler's Lane |
| *Foxglove* , Folk's Glove, Fairy Thimble Fairy Bells | Digitalis – drug used in heart disease. People have been known to drink an infusion of the leaves – highly dangerous. Always grows where the Romans trod. | Cobbler's Lane |
| *St. James Wort* Aaron's Beard Balm for the Warrior's wound | Vulnerary | Cobbler's Lane |
| Gorse 'Never Bloomless' | 'When gorse is out of bloom, kissing's out of tune'. | Cobbler's Lane |

# Appendix 'F'

# Flowers
## (Gathered at Priestley for pressed collection)

### February

Coltsfoot — Name derived from shape of leaves, they could be used for tinder, tho' usually dried to make herb tobacco (mixed with yarrow, rose leaves and sweet herbs for cases of asthma). The corded flowers cure colds and coughs; they were also made into wine. — Sandy spot rear of spinney

### March

Celandine
*Country name:*
Pilewort — Root useful in treating a 'painful disease' — Sunny bank meadow

Red Dead Nettle — — Edge of ploughed field

Ground Ivy
*Country names:*
Gill-run-along
Alehoof
Tunhoof — Remedy for diseases of ear, eye and chest, also coughs and colds. It is boiled in mutton broth for weak and aching backs. Brewers add it to bitter ale to make taste agreeable. — Hedgerow

Wild Arum
*Country names:*
Lords & Ladies
Wake Robin
Angels and Devils
Cuckoo pint
Jack in the pulpit — Floury root used to make starch known as Portland Sago. This was for clear starch, ruffs etc. Berries used as poison. — Hedgerow

### April

a) Scented Blue Violet
b) Scented White Violet — In the time of Charles II the leaves were used for bruises and weak lungs. Flowers made into conserve, violet vinegar or candied. — Hedgerow

White Dead Nettle — Square stem can be made into a musical pipe. Children suck nectar from florets. — Ditch near farm (dry)

147

| | | |
|---|---|---|
| Wild Strawberry | | Bank near farm entrance |
| Jack-by-the-hedge<br>*Country names:*<br>Sauce alone<br>Garlic treacle<br>mustart | Used as a salad herb, boiled as a vegetable made into sauce, like mint sauce. Hot. Very nice. | Hedgerow |
| Moschatel<br>*Country names:*<br>Without Glory<br>Bulbous Fumitory | | Edge of plantation |

**May**

| | | |
|---|---|---|
| Bladder Campion | | Bank near gate |
| Herb Robert<br>(Crane's Bill family)<br>*Country name:*<br>Cranesbill | Flowers all the year round if the weather is right. | Front of farm |
| Creeping Cinquefoil | 'Five-fingered leaf'. Power against evil and witches. | Cornfield |
| Silverweed | Loves the dry dusty places, and the company of man. | Farm track |
| Wood Sorrel | Used for green sauce with the fish course. Juice removes iron mould and spots from linen. Forms a pleasant acid to turn milk into whey for a drink in fevers. | By piece of brickwork |

*Country names:*
The Savoyards (native of Savoy) call it Pain de Dieu (God's bread, or if you like, manna).
Wood Trefoil 'Apothecaries and herbalists call it Alleluya and Cuckowes' meat.

| | | |
|---|---|---|
| a) Germander<br>  Speedwell<br>b) Ivy Leaved<br>  Speedwell<br>*Country names:*<br>a) Bright Eye<br>Paul's Betony | Both flower all through the summer. | Cornfield |
| Cowslip<br>*Country names:*<br>Pretty Mullien<br>Palsywort | Tea from dried flowers, wine from fresh flowers. used as a cosmetic if gathered in dew of early morning. | Grass verge |

148

## June

| | | |
|---|---|---|
| Purple Orchis | | Meadow |

Fumitory — Boiled in whey or milk is used as a cosmetic. Grows where the plough turns, or on fallow leas. — Cornfield
*Country names:*
Fume-de-Terre
Earth smoke

Stichwort — Banks
*Country names:*
Satis Flower, Adder's meat

White Bryony — Young shoots can be eaten as a vegetable, acrid and poisonous as they grow older. Tendrils have gift of twisting different ways. — Hedgerow

Heartsease — Cornfield
*Country names:*
Wild Pansy
Love-in-Idleness
Pink o' my John
Herb Trininty
Lover's thoughts

Dog's Mercury — The spinney

Common Mallow — The seeds we called 'cheeses' — Cornfield

a) Dutch White Clover — The white Dutch Clover always grows in the footprints of the Roman settlers. — a) grass verge
b) Purple Clover — Its treble leaves fold in prayer in heavy dew and rain. — b) cornfield
*Country names:*
a) 'Cloefer Wort' by our ancestors
b) Trefoil

Harebell — The original 'bluebell' of Scotland. Its leaves wither before the flower comes, except for the new ones clustered around the root. This clump was always the first in the district to flower. — By gate entrance to farm from road

Dog Rose — Its hips make a famous cough conserve Rosehip jelly. At the bottom of Creg Hill is the wild white rose which Caesar found and loved when he invaded England. It is the white rose of the Yorkists (War of the Roses). — Hedgerow by wayside
*Country names:*
Rose in dole in
Lancashire
The sweet smelling
one (fragrance
from the leaves is
known as Sweetbriar
or Eglantine

## July

| | | |
|---|---|---|
| Common Avens<br>*Country names*:<br>Blessed Herb<br>Goldy Flower<br>Star of the Earth<br>Herb Bennett | Leaves used as a febrifuge (a medicine which has the property of mitigating a fever). The root has a sweet clove-like odour. Dried, it was laid in chests and drawers to impart its sweet odour to linen. The root also was infused into wine or ale or distilled into 'sweet waters'. When the plant grows in damp places it does not develop its smell. | On the Westoning side |
| Ladies Bedstraw<br>*Country names:*<br>Our Ladies<br>Bead-Straw | This flower is reputed to have burst into bloom on the birth of our Saviour. It was used by many as a rosary, beadlike excrescences frequently appear on the stem. The root gives a red dye, and the flowers will coagulate boiling milk. | Hedgerow |
| Scarlet Pimpernel<br>*Country name:*<br>Shepherd's<br>  weather glass | The old herbalists used it as a cure for many diseases of the brain. It shuts its eye (closes its petals) as a sign of rain. | Cornfield |
| Trailing Vetch | The red pottage for which Esau sold his birthright was made from the seed (lentils) of this vetch. | Roadside |
| Common Red Poppy<br>*Country names:*<br>Headache<br>Cheese bowl | Contains oil in its seeds which is used in cooking and oil painting. | Cornfield |
| Corncockle | Large seed vessel, numerous black glossy seeds. | Cornfield |
| Wild Succory<br>*Country names*:<br>Endive<br>Chicory<br>Keeper of the Ways | It opens its flowers at eight o'clock in the morning, and closes them at four o'clock in the afternoon. | Cornfield |
| Toadflax (yellow)<br>*Country name:*<br>Snapdragon | The juice is expressed and mixed with milk (i) as a cosmetic; (ii) to attract flies! It frequently occurs in the neighbourhood of old monasteries, and appears to have been cultivated by the old monks as a garden flower. | Field track |
| Red Bartsia<br>*Country name:*<br>Brown Weed | | Pastures |

| | | |
|---|---|---|
| Shepherd's Needle<br>*Country name::*<br>Venus Comb | | Cornfield |

**August**

| | | |
|---|---|---|
| Burdock<br>*Country name:*<br>Burrs | The leaves when laid on affected joints relieve rheumatic pain. | Track by buildings |
| Rest Harrow<br>*Country names:*<br>Cammock<br>Landwhin | The roots are sweet and taste of liquorice. | Grassy side of cornfield |
| Large Plantain<br>*Country name:*<br>Englishman's foot | Plaster for broken shins. It is made into many decoctions, washes and applications. Singing birds are fed its brown seeds. | Path |
| Salad Burnett | Leaflets smell and taste of cucumber made into salads its flavour is rather hot. | Pasture |
| Scabious | | Cornfield |
| Kidney Vetch<br>*Country name:*<br>Lamb's toes &<br>ladies' fingers | Plant used as a vulnerary (for groin injury on wounds) and was sold as such in the herb market. | Roadside |
| Forget-me-not | More stories are told about the for-get-me-not, usually the stories and legends are love stories. | Cornfield |
| Nipplewort<br>*Country names:*<br>Swine's Cress<br>Succory Dock<br>Cress | Salad herb – bitter not at all a pleasant flower. | Cornfield |
| Yellow Agrimony | | Hedgerow |
| Goosefoot<br>*Country name:*<br>Good King Henry | Lincolnshire people eat it as spinach which it greatly resembles, with its dull triangular leaves and upright shoots. One of these plants that lurk round the sites of old monasteries, which probably in dearth of other vegetables was cultivated and its insipidity not so much despised. | Near the Westoning end of path |
| Mugwort | Makes a useful tonic, and was worn as a charm against ague. It had a reputation as a preventive of fatigue. | Near a ditch with a brick drain |

**September**

| | | |
|---|---|---|
| Sow Thistle | Rabbit food. | Farm road |
| Stinking Camomile | | Harvested cornfield |
| a) Pink Yarrow<br>b) White Yarrow<br>*Country names:*<br>a) Knighter milfoil<br>b) Soldier's woundwort | Ingredient in herb tobacco, made into ointment. Great reputation as a vulnerary. | Harvested cornfield |
| Selfheal | Famous vulnerary<br>This plant grows plentifully in the neighbourhood of old hermitages and monasteries. | Hedge now bank against holly hedge |

**November**

| | | |
|---|---|---|
| Canker-Rose<br>*Country names:*<br>Fairy Pincushion<br>Rose Sponge | Mossy excrescence on the rose – bramble caused by the gall fly. | Roadside |

# Grasses

| | |
|---|---|
| MEADOW GRASS | Pasture |
| MEADOW FESCUE | Pasture |
| COCK'S FOOT (Dactylis glomerata) | Track |
| DARNELL (Satan Sown) | Cornfield |
| ROUGH BROME GRASS | Among Brambles |
| COMMON SEDGE | Ditch |
| WILD BARLEY or OAT | Path |
| COMMON SEDGE | Ditch |
| SWEET VERNAL | Annual Meadow Grass |
| MEADOW FOXTAIL | Hay Meadow |
| BENTGRASS | Path near Spinney |
| MEADOW SOFT GRASS | Bank near pasture |

# Mosses and Fungi

| | |
|---|---|
| PUFF BALL | In grass |
| COMMON MOSS | (Eurhynchium Praelorgum) base of trees in spinney |
| COMMON MOSS | (Dicronello heteromallo) several cushions, banks, hedgerows etc. |
| HORSETAIL | Boundary between Flitwick Manor and Field. |

Books Published by
# THE BOOK CASTLE

**JOURNEYS INTO HERTFORDSHIRE:** Anthony Mackay
Forword by The Marquess of Salisbury, Hatfield House
Nearly 200 superbly detailed ink drawings depict the towns, buildings and
landscape of this still predominantly rural county.

**JOURNEYS INTO BEDFORDSHIRE:** Anthony Mackay
Foreword by The Marquess of Tavistock, Woburn Abbey
A lavish book of over 150 evocative ink drawings.

**NORTH CHILTERNS CAMERA, 1863–1954; FROM THE
THURSTON COLLECTION IN LUTON MUSEUM:**
edited by Stephen Bunker
Rural landscapes, town views, studio pictures and unique royal portraits by
the area's leading early photographer.

**THROUGH VISITORS' EYES: A BEDFORDSHIRE ANTHOLOGY:**
edited by Simon Houfe
Impressions of the county by famous visitors over the last four centuries,
thematically arranged and illustrated with line drawings.

**FOLK: CHARACTERS and EVENTS in the HISTORY of
BEDFORDSHIRE and NORTHAMPTONSHIRE:** Vivienne Evans
Arranged by village/town, an anthology of stories about the counties' most
intriguing historical figures.

**ECHOES: TALES and LEGENDS of BEDFORDSHIRE and
HERTFORDSHIRE:** Vic Lea
Thirty, compulsively retold historical incidents.

**JOHN BUNYAN: HIS LIFE and TIMES:** Vivienne Evans
Foreword by the Bishop of Bedford
Bedfordshire's most famous son set in his seventeenth century context.

**LOCAL WALKS: NORTH and MID-BEDFORDHSIRE:** Vaughan
Basham
Twenty five circular walks, each linked to an interesting topic.

**LOCAL WALKS: SOUTH BEDFORDSHIRE and NORTH
CHILTERNS:** Vaughan Basham
Twenty seven thematic circular walks.

**CHILTERN WALKS: BUCKINGHAMSHIRE:** Nick Moon
In association with the Chiltern Society, the first of a series of three guides
to the whole Chilterns. Thirty circular walks.

**EVA'S STORY : CHESHAM SINCE the TURN of the CENTURY:**
Eva Rance
The ever-changing twentieth-century, especially the early years at her parents' general stores, Tebby's, in the High Street.

**WHIPSNADE WILD ANIMAL PARK: 'MY AFRICA':** Lucy Pendar
Foreword by Andrew Forbes. Introduction by Gerald Durrell.
Inside story of sixty years of the Park's animals and people – full of anecdotes, photographs and drawings.

**FARM OF MY CHILDHOOD, 1925–1947:** Mary Roberts
An almost vanished lifestyle on a remote farm near Flitwick.

**A LASTING IMPRESSION:** Michael Dundrow
An East End boy's wartime experiences as an evacuee on a Chilterns farm at Totternhoe.

**DUNSTABLE DECADE: THE EIGHTIES** – A collection of photographs:
Pat Lovering
A souvenir book of nearly 300 pictures of people and events in the 1980s.

**DUNSTABLE IN DETAIL:** Nigel Benson
A hundred of the town's buildings and features, plus town-trail map.

**OLD DUNSTABLE:** Bill Twaddle
A new edition of this collection of early photographs.

**BOURNE AND BRED: A DUNSTABLE BOYHOOD BETWEEN THE WARS:** Colin Bourne
An elegantly-written, well-illustrated book capturing the spirit of the town over fifty years ago.

**ROYAL HOUGHTON:** Pat Lovering
Illustrated history of Houghton Regis from the earliest times to the present.

# Specially for Children

**ADVENTURE ON THE KNOLLS: A STORY OF IRON AGE BRITAIN:** Michael Dundrow
Excitement on Totternhoe Knolls as ten-year-old John finds himself back in those dangerous times, confronting Julius Caesar and his army.

**THE RAVENS: ONE BOY AGAINST THE MIGHT OF ROME:** James Dyer
On the Barton hills and in the south-east of England as the men of the great fort of Ravensburgh (near Hexton) confront the invaders.

Further titles are in preparation.
All the above are available via any bookshop, or from the publisher and bookseller

THE BOOK CASTLE
12 Church Street, Dunstable, Bedfordshire LU5 4RU, Tel (0582) 605670